MODERN
TIMES

HEALING OUR CULTURE OF DENIAL, DEPENDENCE, DEBT, AND DECADENCE

W. Michael Campbell, AIA

Published by William Michael Campbell.

Cover design by: Joanne Gibson
Interior design: Claudia Volkman
Editing by: Claudia Volkman

ISBN: 978-1-5323-6811-0

Printed in the United States of America

CONTENTS

INTRODUCTION

FALLEN GIANTS

*"A grove of giant sequoias should be kept just as we keep
a great or beautiful cathedral."*
THEODORE ROOSEVELT

THERE IS A sense of solemnity and stillness in the presence of fallen giants.

Words and pictures simply can never capture the experience of standing at the foot of a giant sequoia in California's Sequoia National Forest. Stable and benevolent giants, these trees have personality, character, and presence. Sequoias are some of the largest and longest living creations on earth.

Along the Trail of 100 Giants, there are three fallen giants: one individual fallen sequoia and a pair that fell together. The pair were the most recent to fall. A German tourist captured the event on his smartphone in 2011. The printed guide gives some clues as to what may have caused them to tumble. A nearby stream may have undermined their surprisingly shallow root system, or it simply may have been old age. You get a better idea of the tremendous scale of these giants when they are lying down and you can climb on top of them and walk end to end. The length of a football field, it reminded me of Gulliver in repose.

One giant resting on its side is estimated to have fallen 160 years ago. The durable wood of the sequoia doesn't show much decay. If I hadn't read the guide, I would have guessed it had been down for only a decade or two.

Another fallen giant is hidden by overgrowth, covered by moss, and partially rotted away. This giant must have come to rest here hundreds of years ago. I couldn't help but grab a few broken branches to take home as a souvenir.

The fall of these giants must have been very violent. People within a mile or so would have thought they were experiencing an earthquake. Now there is only quiet and the sound of the wind through the branches.

To be standing in the Forum in Rome, Italy, is to be in the presence of another fallen giant, the once grand and mighty Roman Empire.

There are architectural giants here. Some are still standing, but most have fallen. One temple marauders tried to topple is still standing; now it is a Christian church. The method of demolishing these buildings was to create a small notch at the top of the columns. Marauders would then begin drawing a large rope back and forth over this notch, adding sand for an abrasive. By standing on the ground and drawing the rope back and forth, a diagonal groove would develop and deepen until the stone column was weakened to the point of collapse. In the case of this particular temple, the harder stone of the columns discouraged the vandals, and they moved on.

Just as with the fall of the giant sequoias, the fall of the Roman Empire was very violent. Much like the pair of giants that fell in 2011, the Roman Empire was undermined and eroded below for a long period of time before it fell.

Aside from the diagonal scars on the temple columns that resisted demolition, there is not much today that conveys the violence that took place here as Rome was overrun successively by hordes of vandals. Not much tells us of the discord and chaos that preceded the fall, the generations of decline, and the decadence. Now there is just the whine of Vespas in the background.

The Forum is now a place of calm and safety. Walking with my daughter through these ruins, there is no sense of being in danger. That's how it would have been during Rome's days of ascendance, strength, and stability. This was followed by a long, slow period of decline. Generations of Roman life were characterized by *denial, debt, dependence*, and *decadence*. The governing class was increasingly less equipped to truly lead and instead catered to mob rule. A long period of dullness, violence, and discord took place within before Rome was destroyed from without.

The United States of America is a giant of an empire too. No longer can we claim to be similar to the stable and benevolent giant sequoia. Now we are more like the Roman Empire heading for its fall. We, too, are characterized by *denial, dependence, debt,* and *decadence*. We are in that state of instability and dullness that precedes the much more tangible violence that accompanies the fall of a giant.

Once a giant sequoia begins to list and fall, there is no way to stop it from crashing down to the forest floor; the mass and momentum are too great. It is not always so with great empires. It is rare, but nations *can* reverse their decline. There is historical evidence that societies can reform themselves by returning to a few simple, timeless ideals, precepts, and proverbial wisdom.

In the days of Rome's ascendance, their citizens never imagined that a classic, multivolume history known as *The Decline and Fall of the Roman Empire* would ever be written about them. Can we imagine that someday there will be a history book called *The Decline and Fall of the United States of America*? It might happen sooner rather than later if we as a nation don't completely change course.

There are solutions. God created us and the world around us that way. Because of that we should never be without hope and direction. He has given us a world of problems and solutions, deceit and truth, vice and virtue, sin and redemption, pride and humility. We simply need to acknowledge our true faults and failings at this time in history and turn to the simple principles, precepts, and laws of His creation.

We have to acknowledge that we have become a culture of *denial, dependence, debt,* and *decadence*. *Denial* of the very sad and sick state of our culture and the failings of man centered solutions. *Debt* and bankruptcy at all levels—not just fiscal but spiritual as well. Misplaced *dependencies* and all form and manner of addictions. We are a *decadent* society that has replaced the principles of wisdom, prudence, sacrifice, and true respect for all the lives around us with the principle of pleasure and expediency, regardless of the cost to the innocent lives that are harmed by this behavior.

The solutions are simple but not easy. There are manmade and spiritual forces that are powerfully and firmly entrenched against a solution. The greatest death knell to these forces is honesty. If we can honestly admit and accept the state we are in and identify the real causes, then solutions and power will flow to us naturally. If we can be honest about the true motives of the suppliers and receivers of dependence, we can wean ourselves of these morbid dependencies and restore our pride, our self-esteem, and our coffers. If we can turn from inordinate demands for pleasure and entertainment to some higher principles to motivate us, then we can achieve real peace and true brotherhood in our society.

Centuries from now a father and daughter might walk through the ruins of one of our great cities and somberly meditate on what a great, tragic, and unnecessary fall took place. Empires don't last forever, it's true. Someday future generations will look on the remnants of our great culture with wonder, but that fall does not have to happen here and now. It doesn't have to be by our own hands. Embracing a few timeless ideals, a few basic precepts, and some proverbial wisdom can remove the pall that is over us and restore our flagging empire.

We are in a state of decline. This cannot be denied, but we need not despair. Facing our societal problems honestly and acting with humility, wisdom, faith, hope, and charity will cause them to recede. Adopting a few timeless spiritual principles will heal our culture.

Giant sequoias should be preserved. Majestic cathedrals should be restored. Great republics should be restored and preserved as well.

"This is their temple, vaulted high,
And here we pause with reverent eye,
With silent tongue and awe-struck soul;
For here we sense life's proper goal.
To be like these, straight, true and fine,
To make our world, like theirs a shrine;
Sink down, O traveler, on your knees,
God stands before you in these trees."
JOSEPH B. STRAUSS, FROM "THE REDWOODS," 1932

ONE

MODERN TIMES

"Dear Lord God, Make me a bird, so I can fly far, far away."
JENNIE, FROM FORREST GUMP

MANY OF US have experienced a dark day in their lives—that day when things suddenly go horribly wrong. I was twelve when I had such a day. I didn't become a man that day, but I stopped being a child.

Up to that point life had been full of wonder. I grew up in the 1960s in suburban New Jersey. It wasn't the sixties you see in documentaries, with rampant drugs, sex, and radicalism. The sixties I knew consisted of quiet, prosperous Main Streets without the ever-present crackle and buzz that is in the air almost everywhere today. My siblings and I could ride for miles on our bikes to the local hobby shops and surrounding woods. No one wore helmets. As long as we were home before the street lights came on, there wasn't much for our parents to worry about. They made sure we stayed out of the low-income, high-crime areas in our town and didn't ride our mini bikes in the streets, instead walking them to the trails in the woods. Other than that, we had very few boundaries. Our culture at the time did not require them. Our world was simple, quiet, and safe.

To all outward appearances, my siblings and I enjoyed an enviable lifestyle. The white fence that bounded our quarter-acre property was always freshly painted. We had a perfect lawn without a single weed. We all appeared to be doing very well. I always looked neat and clean at school or play. I scored the highest on my sixth grade aptitude tests. The prettiest and smartest girl in class was my first crush, and I hoped I was hers. My siblings and I all looked like children from a good family with promising futures.

My father was an FBI agent in one of the New York City field offices. He was a Cold War soldier who was passionately against anything to do with socialism here and abroad. I have a newspaper clipping of him escorting a suspect into court. A signed photograph of J. Edgar Hoover sat on the bookshelf in our living room. My father hated all things liberal. He would yell at the television during election coverage. I only had a vague understanding of what was so upsetting to him. My mother told me years later when she saw me reading the *New York Times* that my father refused to allow that paper in our house when he was alive.

My father was what we would call strict back then. My hair was kept short. If I came home from the barber with my hair touching my ears or collar, I was sent back to get it cut again. An aunt had given me some money to go clothes shopping when we visited her. I came home with a Nehru jacket that promptly had to be returned. My surfer's cross also didn't last very long—my father informed me that it was the same as the iron cross worn by the Nazis. He tried to protect me from all the things that he feared and hated, but the explanation about the surfer's cross was as far as he ever came to explaining to me *why* he felt as strongly as he did.

Maybe some of it was rebellion against that same aunt, his mother's sister. She was the family matriarch, a lifelong New Deal Democrat who was heavily involved in the party. She was the first woman to speak at the Democratic National Convention, and she co-chaired the 1964 Democratic National Convention with Lady Bird Johnson. One family story has it that the phone rang during dinner at her home, and one of her black maids told the caller, "Mrs. Sharp is not taking calls at this time." My aunt was horrified that her maid had just hung up on Jackie Kennedy. She scrambled to return the call and make amends.

My aunt held a position in state government as the head of Civil Service. She never had children of her own and was widowed before I was born. Her husband had been a successful career politician as well. She was the only wealthy relative we had, and trips to her house were always a delight. It was a one block walk to the shops on Landis Avenue, and she would supply funds for our excursions. Dinner was always in the dining room with her household help preparing and serving dinner. A crystal bell sat on the table for us to ring if we needed anything, though my mother, the daughter of Depression-Era farmers, discouraged us from using it.

She had a chauffeur provided by the state who would pick us up and take us to visit her office a few doors down from the governor, overlooking the rotunda of the State House. Then the chauffeur would take us on a trip to Atlantic City to the arcades and rides there.

Her whole life had been spent in politics. Born forty or fifty years later, she would have been in a position similar to that of Nancy Pelosi or Hillary Rodham Clinton. As she got older and early signs of dementia set in, she lost her influence. Those in power, or seeking to be, no longer came to meet in her parlor to seek her influence and intervention. Toward the end of her life, she was no longer able to recognize anyone. When I visited her in the nursing home, she seemed burdened with guilt. The last time I saw her, she was staring at nothing in particular and repeating over and over, "I told him not to do it; I told him not to do it."

Another one of my paternal ancestors going back five generations was Dr. James Parkinson. While he was active in politics, he is best known as the doctor that identified the disease that was named for him, although his work wasn't recognized until almost one hundred years after his death. His interests were in social and political concerns as well as medicine and paleontology, and he wrote about all four. I have two of his books in my library: *Shaking Palsy* and *The Village Friend*. The second was written to teach the poor about basic health maintenance and first aid. One of his prescriptions for health was reading the Bible daily.

As I got older, our home changed; It became a sick and violent place. My father had become a violent alcoholic by the time I was eleven. He had left the FBI to start his own law practice, and it was failing.

In spite of this there is much that I look back on with gratitude. I enjoyed church. I enjoyed the music and messages and remember vividly that feeling of walking out of church on a spring morning with that feeling of being clean inside and out. I loved everything about belonging to the Boy Scouts—the hiking, camping, and picnics. I lost myself in wood lore, knot tying, wood carving, and the Pinewood Derby.

I still have a hard time sorting out how what had happened that one very dark night. For a week my mother had been trying to talk to my father. His snub-nosed .38 service pistol on the end table, I remember my mother trying to take it away from him and him taking it back. Lying in bed that evening, I heard the shot.

Some can understand the confusion I felt. Hearing the shot, feeling tension leave my body, the relief that he was gone. *It's over.* Then being overwhelmed with guilt for feeling relieved. I then convinced myself that wasn't really what happened—he was just throwing furniture at the walls again. He had done that before. I fell asleep and woke up to the horrific sound of my mother screaming, "He did it; he did it!" She called a neighbor, and soon the police and ambulances arrived. I didn't come down from my room that day. I watched through the window from the top of my bunk bed. The ambulance, police, and their photographer came and went. I watched as they rolled my world away on a sheet-covered stretcher.

Life continued as before for a little while. Up to this point, to all outward appearances we had a very normal looking, prosperous life. But now my friends' parents didn't allow them to come over anymore. On my first birthday party after the suicide, not one invited friend showed up, not one.

Anger, a pervasive sadness, and pessimism settled down deep inside of me. The soul-starving attitudes of bitterness and self-pity took hold. Coupled with a stoicism and intellectual pride, I had little in the way of spiritual health to pull me up and out of the mire I was in.

My mom escaped into her own world of alcoholism. My siblings and I to fend for ourselves as best we could.

I didn't know much about the 70's counterculture world into which I escaped. I had no notion whatsoever back then that maybe this new exotic lifestyle was the result of any particular ideology or movement. I thought all of this just came about spontaneously. I did not see it as the result of some design or purposeful political cause promoted by people with an agenda of their own. I thought I was being free, rebellious, and independent, when actually I was being controlled and manipulated by those with an activist mentality. I just knew that, at least for the moment, it provided a place of comfort and distraction. I didn't have the faintest notion that there were people with an agenda that had designs on my life.

My father had been an excellent woodworker. It wasn't something we shared or that he taught me. He was solitary in almost everything he did.

After he died, I inherited his wood shop, complete with the band saw, table saw, wood lathe, and other tools.

Rather than perfectly crafted colonial replicas that he created, I began to craft the hardware of my new lifestyle. These were not the ordinary "bongs" found in head shops. These were crafted on a wood lathe and about eight inches long. I made them in different materials and stain colors. The ebony model with the leather grip was the most popular.

When someone first embarks on a life of sickness and misplaced dependencies, there is a honeymoon phase. There are feelings of adventure, energy, freedom, and even euphoria. Years later, even though I can look back and see the misery that followed, I still have fond memories of that initial departure from a real and functional life. Sitting under a tree in the woods smoking pot in the afternoon seemed free and natural. I was unaware of the snares that would grab hold of me and take me places I didn't want to go. As with the beginning of any unwholesome dependence, I thought all my problems and burdens had been lifted. In truth they were growing and gaining strength while I looked the other way. In reality I was only putting off dealing with the real issues and depleting the reserves of youth at an accelerated pace.

By the time I entered high school, I was what any outside observer would have called a burnout. Long hair, acne problems, and socially awkward, especially when it came to connecting with the opposite sex.

Initially I didn't have any thoughts of going to college, but a few people in my life encouraged me. A girlfriend of mine was a cheerleader, and she cheered me on and encouraged me to take my SATs and apply to colleges.

Because of my past academic achievements, I was assigned to advanced placement classes in high school. For AP Physics in my senior year, I had a teacher named Mr. Scharmann. He reminded me of a bombastic Santa Claus. He frequently called me to the board to solve the problem of the day. He saw something in me and knew how to get it out of me. "Mr. Campbell," he would say, "I know you've got some smarts in you, and I'm going to get them out." His lessons later served me well in college when I took structural engineering classes.

When most of the people in your life are as sick and self-centered as you are, the acceptance and encouragement of a few means a great deal and can carry you a long way. The acceptance and encouragement of my girlfriend, Mr. Scharmann, and others changed my life, though it would take a few more years and a power greater than human encouragement to turn me around.

Gradually the idea of becoming an architect took hold of me. I made more than bongs in that wood shop—I also designed and built real furniture. Furniture is merely small architecture, and I simply grew from designing and building furniture to designing buildings. I enjoyed the architectural part of the mechanical drawing classes I took, even though the teacher was not very encouraging. He pronounced the class "mechanical drawling," and he didn't like my designs. I would go to the library and check out books on furniture design, architecture, and building, and then I would fail to return them. I recently came across some of those books and took them back to their respective libraries. No one has contacted me yet to let me know what forty years of library late charges comes out to.

Once I set my sights on college, I would not be deterred. I found out years later that my mother and I had the same story. We had both been told by guidance counselors that we did not have the abilities to go into our chosen fields of study. We both remembered that at that very moment we decided we would succeed just because they said we couldn't.

Because of my poor academic performance in high school, I couldn't go directly to a school of architecture. Most have higher entrance standards than a typical liberal arts school. Because I had been in AP classes, I had completed most of the requirements for high school graduation by the beginning of my senior year and wasn't very motivated to show up after that point. My transcript showed a C average and more days absent than present. It would require more than wishful thinking to accomplish my goals; it would require work. I went to a junior college and got my GPA up over 3.5 and started the application process over again.

I was accepted to Louisiana State University's School of Architecture in the middle of my second year and boarded a Greyhound bus headed for Baton Rouge from Penn Station in New York City. After the first few hours I realized that this bus was a local bus, not an express. For two-and-a-half days, we stopped at every small town along the way. A Greyhound bus is not very pleasant after a few days. Before I even got off the bus in Baton Rouge, I had already hooked up with another druggie heading to LSU.

I went by cab from the Baton Rouge bus station to the dorm I was going to be staying in, West Hall. As I stepped out of the cab, it suddenly hit me that I didn't know a single soul within twelve hundred miles.

My first roommate at West Hall had a bookcase full of books by and about Billy Graham. I had arrived and set up for the semester while he was out for the weekend. The first time he walked into the room to meet his new roommate, I had Black Sabbath blasting on the stereo. This roommate was one more person that was accepting and very tolerant of me and my lifestyle.

I'm pretty sure he had his whole church praying for me.

I led two lives at LSU. Studying architecture gave me purpose and a sense of belonging. Architecture studio design labs are famous for long hours and pulling overnighters to meet project deadlines. Such an atmosphere created friendships that have lasted for thirty-five years. Compared to my troubled background, the lives of the other architecture students seemed normal and problem-free. Most seemed to come from strong, supportive families. Over the years, I would realize that this wasn't entirely the case, but their lives were still a world away from my other friends. The architecture students were mostly conservative as far as I could tell, but they accepted me as I was nonetheless. Sometimes I think they just didn't know what to make of me and my behavior and attitudes.

The other world I lived in, mostly on weekends, was the world of drug dealers and users in Baton Rouge and New Orleans. I always managed to have money for alcohol and somehow managed to have access to large amounts of expensive drugs. This was a world far removed from my true self. Three-day cocaine binges without any sleep. Cocaine to get up and Quaaludes to try and get back down. My friends and I holed up in a shotgun house in New Orleans with large zip lock bags full of coke. Feeling like an alien walking on another planet when I had to leave and walk around the corner for more Dixie beer.

My summer construction job was with another drug dealer. Most of my fellow laborers were part of that circle and most had been shot at least once. One worker, "Big Saul," had been shot seven times with a .45 by a jealous girlfriend and lived through it. When a friend didn't show up for work one day, it didn't cause much of a stir with the other workers when it was found out he had been shot and killed in his sleep the night before for a bag of Quaaludes.

Ronald Reagan came to the LSU campus during the 1980 presidential campaign. Being the hippie type that I was, I knew that this was probably an evil man, but I went to hear him for what I thought would be entertainment value. I stood in an aisle with my backpack on and my back to a wall. A serious looking man with aviator glasses took up position next to me. The radical student groups were all there with their banners, shouting and heckling. I was very impressed by how pointed but good-natured Reagan's responses were to them. Walking back into the architecture studio later that day, I announced to everyone that he was such a good speaker that he could almost get someone like me to vote for him. A few years later I was standing in line at the student union when news of an assassination attempt played on the screen. I walked back to the architecture studio, and in a heartless tone told my fellow students, "Someone shot Reagan." I had a different response years later when I heard of his death. At the time of his speech, I was completely unaware of how his successful life would eventually help make my own life more successful.

A few years ago, I was stuck in traffic outside the Lincoln Tunnel heading into Manhattan. The cause of the backup became apparent when a line of black SUVs with darkened windows passed alongside me. Another presidential candidate was leaning out an open window, waving to onlookers, a handsome young man with a broad grin. I didn't realize at the time that this man's success at winning elections would make providing for my family more challenging.

In spite of a growing dependence on drugs and alcohol, I did manage to push ahead and sometimes even excel in my classes at LSU. I graduated on the dean's list my final year.

In 1982, the year I graduated, I came back home to New Jersey and started looking for work in New York City. At the time we were still in the economic malaise created in the 70s. Hundreds of resumes produced a handful of interviews, but none that led to a job. Showing up to interviews with alcohol on my breath did not help. I finally managed to get a position at a local firm, working for the minimum wage with no benefits.

By now, my drinking had become all-consuming. I would start drinking before getting out of bed in the morning and continue that way throughout the day. The office I worked in was pretty empty, so it wasn't too hard to smuggle my bottle in. I couldn't imagine life without alcohol, but I couldn't imagine living this way either. I found myself on the basement stairs of my mother's house one day, contemplating the same end as my father.

I knew I had to stop running. Years of deferred maintenance on my life brought me to the point of not being able to function or cope on my own. I hadn't thought of God for many years, but that day I offered up a simple, earnest prayer: "Help!"

The purveyors of modernist thought, humanists, naturalists, and progressives have proclaimed that "God is dead"; I found them to be wrong. My prayer was answered with power, guidance, provision, mercy, and grace.

I was at the point of despair. I was physically and mentally ill. But it was as if a powerful hand had taken hold of the back of my shirt collar, lifted me up, set me on my feet, and guided me in the direction I needed to go.

As a child I had faith. I had a sense that God cared for me, that He worked in my life in small and big ways. I didn't worry; I knew He would provide. I was not overly troubled when I saw injustice because I knew that eventually, given time, that God would bring about the consequences that were deserved. I felt He had a design and good purpose for my life. It wasn't a mature faith, but it was an optimistic and sunny faith. That faith wasn't destroyed that tragic night when I was twelve; it was just misplaced. Without any hope in my soul for so long, I simply didn't think I had any options. I had forgotten about God for a time, but He hadn't forgotten about me.

I began to get help, and I started sorting things out. It had been ten years of drugs and alcohol, misery and depression, but now I was free. A sense of hope and faith took root again, deep down inside me.

Up to that point my life had been controlled by four characteristics that held me: *denial, dependence, debt,* and *decadence.*

I was in *denial* regarding the real source of my problems, and I was unable to be honest with myself. But somehow, deep inside, I was inspired to get real, and this began to propel me toward a solution.

My life was full of misplaced *dependencies* on other people, drugs, and alcohol. I had a general sense that others should take care of me—that I was the needy one. Turning from morbid dependencies on alcohol and people to vital dependencies on God and the love of people of true good will restored my sense of self.

I was in *debt*—morally, emotionally, mentally, and financially. I was not taking care of myself or meeting my responsibilities. I was a taker, not a giver. In my new life I quickly became debt-free and began to find ways to give rather than take.

My life was characterized by *decadence*—in the true meaning of the word, not how we think of it today. Decadence simply means to be in a state of decline. I experienced a long series of cowardly decisions to choose short-term gratification over facing into my mounting personal problems in order to turn things around. Turning to spiritual and moral principles for living, I began to build a life of structure and purpose rather than destructive self-gratification.

I am still a very imperfect person, but the above characteristics began to reverse after my experience of grace. To some extent, they naturally seemed to fade. In other ways it continues to be an ongoing battle to overcome these negative traits, as it is for many, but the consequences of not dealing with them is going back to the way I was.

Our culture at this time is not so unlike the state I was in before my experience of grace. We are characterized by *denial, dependence, debt,* and *decadence.* The solutions to these besetting problems are the same for society as they were for me.

Honestly admitting my faults and failings and adopting a few simple, spiritual principles restored my life and the lives of those around me.

The simple spiritual principles that work to restore the life of an individual will work to restore a family, a community, a city, or a nation. Being completely truthful with ourselves and acting in wisdom, faith, hope, and charity will reverse the state of decline we are in and restore real peace to our land. There was hope for me, and there is hope for our culture.

"Faith never knows where it is being led,
but it loves and knows the One who is leading."
OSWALD CHAMBERS

TWO
SIGNS OF THE TIMES

"With God's help I shall now become myself."
SØREN KIERKEGAARD

I AM A different person now. My thinking has changed on so many levels. I simply returned to the person I was intended to be all along: my true self.

Now most of my working days are spent as an architect designing new churches and restoring old ones. This is my area of specialization and expertise, and it is what I delight in doing.

There is a lot about buildings that can give us life lessons both by how they come together and by how they fall apart. Likewise the building and architectural process can be used to illustrate thoughts on life and the culture around us. Following in this chapter and others are illustrations from architecture applied to our culture and how it can come together or crumble and fall apart.

Many of the denominational churches that I work with are struggling. Their old buildings are deteriorating, and their congregations are dwindling. They all have similar histories: Times of growth and vitality fifty or a hundred years ago, followed by declining attendance, shrinking memberships, and aging congregations. I get involved when the masonry starts to crumble and the roofs of these wonderful old structures begin to leak. Sometimes I am called in to make these buildings accessible for members that are starting to have trouble with the stairs.

During the planning and budgeting process, the topic of shrinking congregations often comes up and a few opinions are thrown out as to why things are the way they are. It is usually attributed to changing demographics, lifestyles, and so on—"natural changes, out of our control." Often beneath the hopeful promise of restoration and drawing people back to the church is a sense of desperation.

For instance, one of my projects in central New Jersey was a grand old church built over one hundred years ago. Two decades after the original construction, there was a catastrophic fire. About 25 percent of the original brownstone walls remained after the fire. The restoration of the surviving structure was built using cast stone, a new man-made material being developed at the time. The cast stone manufactured today is a close match visually to real stone and will last indefinitely. Cast stone in the 1920s, however, was a poorer quality cinder aggregate material. Usually the molds were packed with a half-inch thick layer of better quality material that would be the finished face of the product. The balance of the mold was then filled with the cheaper concrete material. Over time small breaches in this finished material would allow moisture into the core material, and deterioration would begin to accelerate. Like the basement walls of houses built in the 1920s, this material starts to crumble after a few decades.

Most of the time when I come across this problem, it involves just a few of the ornamental details and spires. In the case of this church, however, almost the entire facade was made of this material and had deteriorated. Correcting this is a massive project far beyond the financial means of the church. Even in its heyday this would have been a daunting project, but now the one thousand-seat sanctuary has under 150 congregants in attendance on a Sunday morning.

One sunny fall day, I walked around, attempting to survey the condition of the structure. It is necessary to spend a lot of time with a building to really understand the nature and scope of the problems and the required remedial work. Spending time around old artifacts and old buildings often gives me a sense of melancholy. I experience sadness for some quality or characteristic of the people or their time that has been lost. It's not romanticism; it's a true grieving for real qualities of life that once were but are no longer common for us.

Once this had been a thriving and affluent parish. Now facing the reality of the depressed state of both the buildings and the congregation, the gray emptiness of it all reminded me of churches in socialist or former Soviet states. I began to think that maybe this congregation's problems weren't so different from congregations in those countries. Perhaps the same forces that emptied the churches of Eastern Europe were at work here. What if it wasn't the result of some natural cultural shift or spontaneous social change, but instead a concerted effort to remake our culture—and in particular our churches?

As my forebears were, I have been involved in politics and social concerns. At one time, I was very emotionally involved with one view, and now I see things from what would be called a more classical view. Walking around that church that day, it became clear to me that there is a common pedigree to the ideology that dominates our culture and the laws, policies, and values that spring from it. Many may disagree, but I believe there are common threads woven throughout the dominant ideologies of our time, and the precepts of those common threads are very simple. One common thread is rejecting the idea of a sovereign God and adopting the belief that the "wisdom of man" is supreme. This rejection of timeless wisdom and instead man relying on his own devices is called by many names, but that only serves to confuse. For the purposes of this book, there is one simple heading: *modernism*.

When I undertake a restoration project, I start with a "conditions report."The church leaders know there are problems, but they don't really know the cause or extent of the problems. They know that the roof leaks and there are pieces of stone and slate landing on the sidewalk around the building, but my team goes over the building from top to bottom and from the outside in. We look at all the structural, mechanical, and architectural systems. We put our findings into a bound report outlining what's wrong, what needs to be done to correct the problems, and how much it will cost. We prioritize the work that is to be done. Some projects need to be addressed immediately because they pose a threat to the safety of the members of the church or they are seeming small problems that have the potential to become very big problems. It is a sometimes unpleasant task to be the bearer of bad news. Being that I was invited to do this work and there was some acknowledgment of the problems before calling me, my assessment is usually graciously and courageously received. It would be different if the news was unsolicited.

Like the physical structure of the church, the ideology that has infiltrated and undermined the church and the culture around it has a sound-looking finish. This finish veneer is pigmented, sculpted, and textured to look like real stone. It looks solid, and we have trusted in it. At its core, though, it has no real substance, no real load-bearing capacity. It cannot hold up over time to bear the loads it is intended to carry. It is not the rock we should place our foundation on.

It is not out of willful ignorance that many people don't see the problems in their buildings. They don't have the training or the calling to do this work. They are there to worship and participate in other church programs, not survey masonry conditions. For example, one church was at an intersection I often stopped at. While waiting for traffic to clear, I would always glance at the corner spire of this church, which was leaning about five degrees out of plumb. I always wondered if it would topple over. Eventually I was hired to work on this church. I made my presentation, mentioning this condition to the committee. They were all surprised—they had never noticed it before.

Like my clients with their buildings, many of us don't have the time or inclination to look at what's really going on around us. We don't really attempt to delve into the heart of what's wrong with our world today, even when we know something is very wrong. The roof is leaking and the structure of our culture is falling down around us. While many are vested in the problems, others are willfully ignorant. Most of us, though, are simply burdened with the responsibilities and struggles of life and do not have the wherewithal to take on anymore. It is also very unsettling to look at the problems mounting around us. It requires courage and inspiration beyond our own limited perceptions to face these things squarely. It requires God's help to see the truth of our situation at this time in history.

There has been a revolution in our culture over the past several generations: For the first time in the history of the world, men and women collectively—almost universally—have put aside God and substituted the will and "wisdom" of man. Flawed humans have arrogantly set themselves up as the ultimate authority over creation and each other. This was Adam and Eve's original temptation: to be like God and assume to know all things.

These changes have come at us one sound bite at a time, one emotional argument after another. In the constant buzz it is hard to see the big picture. What belief systems are our cultural changes and new laws derived from? What is their source? Where have they been implemented before, and what were the consequences?

What is the driving force of our times? It no longer appears to be the spirit of 1776, with limited government and individual liberty. And it's also not traditional, orthodox religion, Eastern or Western.

What worldview is shaping how we live? It used to be the founding principles of our country. Now that only seems to be given lip service and sentimental recognition, but it's no longer the impetus behind shaping decisions. And what has happened to the worldview that we are all created in the image and likeness of our Creator and that *all* are precious in His sight? That idea, too—at least in popular culture—is shunned rather than embraced.

A movement can have many characteristics, as well as many false ways of portraying itself, but just a few defining traits or one primary trait they are truly characterized by. A person may speak the truth most of the time, but, if in those critical moments that test character, he is dishonest, then you would say he is dishonest. If a person or organization shows courage and honesty in those defining moments, you would say they are honest and courageous. If a person or organization claims to derive their inspiration from one source, yet their actions consistently show another motivation, you would have to say they are motivated by the latter. Modernists may claim a faith or patriotic inspiration, but their actions will tell if that is true or if their inspiration is atheistic, self-willed, and self-centered—or even malevolent.

The dominant forces in today's world have certain common characteristics. If we are honest they are fairly easy to see. But since they're not very attractive to look at, they are usually cloaked in some seductive and enticing garment. In actuality, though, these forces are the same beliefs and characteristics that brought to ruin civilizations from the beginning of history.

But while these characteristics are fairly easy to observe, they are not easy to look at. At first, like many of the congregations I work with, many of us would rather not look at the truth of what is going on around us. We may have come to place our emotional or financial security in these unsustainable systems and beliefs, and now we are unable to resist the modernism that is subtly pulling us into chaos and destruction.

I use the term *modernism* to encompass the common set of core principles and behaviors in all the humanist and atheistic belief systems. Communism, socialism, national socialism, liberalism, and progressivism all spring from the same root, sharing the same common threads woven throughout.

Modernism in this sense does not refer to sleek and unadorned designs without ornamentation or the marvels of technology; instead it refers to the ideology and dogma of humanism and secularism. It comes down to basic beliefs about the nature of man, God, and Truth. The modernist believes that man is a soulless, evolved being. The modernist believes that there is no sovereign God. The modernist believes there is no ultimate Truth.

Some modernists may appear to believe that we are created beings, that there is a God, and that there are certain truths, but the willfulness of their actions deny these things. All modernist movements at their heart are based on the belief that man alone is sovereign, God (if there is a God) is made in man's image, and truth is ultimately of man's determination.

There are really only a few worldviews that are dominant in the world today. For the most part, culturally we are in an anti-Christian age where socialism and humanism—i.e., modernism—drive culture and legislation.

You can consider the following chapters as one man's "conditions report"—an assessment of what ails us in these times, and what steps we can take to make changes before it is too late.

We should not be without hope. There are solutions to our problems. As complex and overwhelming as they may appear, there are simple principles that will restore our culture and our communities. Facing our problems honestly and moving forward with humility, wisdom, faith, hope, and charity will remove our fears and give us strength and clear direction.

As a people we have not truly been ourselves for some time now. If we will simply turn to our Creator and His ways, He will do the rest and restore us to our true selves. We have forgotten about God for a time, but He has not forgotten about us or His love for us.

"When we advance confidently in the direction of our dreams, and endeavor to live the life which we have imagined, we will meet with success unexpected in common hours. We will put some things behind and will pass an invisible boundary. New, universal, and more liberal laws will begin to establish themselves around and within us, and the old laws will be expanded and interpreted in our favor. And we will live with the freedom of a higher order of beings."
HENRY DAVID THOREAU, ADAPTED

THREE

WHAT HAS CHANGED?

"Yes, this desire to stifle the voice of God is rather well planned. Many will do just about anything so that His voice will not be heard, so that only the voice of man will be heard, a voice that has nothing to offer except the things of this world. And sometimes such an offer brings with it destruction of cosmic proportions. Isn't this the tragic history of our century?"
ST. JOHN PAUL II, CROSSING THE THRESHOLD OF HOPE

WE ALL HAVE our own point of view of what the "good old days" looked like. Those of us whose memories and experiences reach back to the mid-sixties have a unique perspective on history; our coming of age coincided with dramatic changes in our culture's beliefs and the tone and tenor of the world around us.

There was chaos in my own household when I was growing up, but there was a general peace and stability in the world outside. Things were quieter then. There was less discord and much less violence. There wasn't such a pervasive sense of anxiety. Of course there were dysfunctional families like mine. There have always been young people in our schools that were on the fringe. In the sixties, I knew other kids who were troubled and from obviously troubled families, but they didn't bring guns to school and start shooting their classmates and teachers.

The weapons that have been used in school shootings are not new. The patents for these firearms are a hundred years old. Gun laws have changed, becoming much more restrictive. At one time, in some states an adult could walk into a hardware store and buy a fully automatic

Thompson submachine gun with no background check. And yet there weren't any mass murders at our schools and shopping centers back then. So what has changed?

Our culture is what has changed. It hasn't been a natural evolution or cultural shift; it's been by design. The change has come about from the activism of a relatively small group of people with a well-orchestrated plan to change how we view ourselves, others, creation, and God Himself.

Previous generations had a somewhat unified and classical view of right and wrong and a common view of a God watching over us and giving us precepts to follow. We now have a disintegrated culture filled with images of violence and death and almost infinite individual definitions of what is right and wrong, good and bad. Our leaders, and those in media, express outrage over random killings and demand action, but then make ambiguous statements about the value of *all* human life and no longer protect the most fragile among us. *Leadership matters,* and when our leaders have such torturously confused ideas about the value of human life, at all stages and in all circumstances. When these leaders defend and even advocate for the most barbaric destruction and exploitation of innocent human life, we shouldn't be surprised when the weak and unstable among us go over the edge and act out in violence.

These tragedies are not the result of a lack of new laws. If we can't give our youth a clear view of right and wrong and some hope in things beyond the material, there can never be enough laws to contain the confused and violent fallout.

If the eminent collapse of an empire were evident to all, cultures would never decline and collapse. The Roman Empire would rule the world today. Those in our culture who warn us of the dangerous state we are in are scorned, which is the very nature of a culture in decline. There is a point of no return—when the besetting problems reach critical mass, only complete collapse and the clarity of hindsight will show what should have been obvious all along.

Because of our refusal to acknowledge the severity of our problems and their true source, and then to follow a few basic, timeless principles, we are storing up great trouble for ourselves. But it doesn't have to be this way.

We need not be discouraged. Buildings and works of art can be restored. We see it all the time. Our society can be restored too. A few simple virtues will restore our strength and build a culture that men and women of good will would be proud to pass on to the next generation.

If we have become a culture characterized by *denial, dependence, debt,* and *decadence,* what is it that we have lost and need to be restored to?

Virtues to Regain

Sincerity

I've heard it said that when a word describing a negative characteristic falls from use, it's because that characteristic is in abundance. *Guile* is such a word. It means "to promote selfish gain by artful or cunning deceit." The opposite of guile is *sincerity.* As the old joke goes: "Being a good salesman is all about sincerity. Once you can fake that, the rest is easy." I think this well describes many of our current leaders. They are full of guile and lacking real sincerity but doing a masterful job of faking it. Modernists mistakenly see guile as sophistication.

Being without guile or being sincere means to have purity and unselfishness of purpose. To be sincere we also need the virtues of *courage* and *honesty.* We often talk of honor, courage, and sacrifice in regard to our military and first responders, but it is needed as much, if not more, in our political leaders. It is needed in our day-to-day lives and when we go to the voting booth. If you think about it, you would be hard-pressed to find an example of real courage and selfless behavior amongst our elected officials. Sincerity needs to be part of a leader's earliest choices to seek office. Once a person has compromised themselves, even in a small way, it is nearly impossible to get back to a position of sincerity. As with all matters related to our cultural restoration, it needs to start with us—the ordinary people.

Sincerity amongst ourselves and in our leaders will bring light to our neighborhoods, our state and national capitols, and break the chains and shackles of *denial* that are dragging us to places we shouldn't go. Another word that has fallen from use that describes a negative characteristic of our culture is farcical.

Vitality

Vitality means "to be full of life; life-giving." A similar word is *inspired*—which is to be "full of the Spirit." If our dependencies are vital, full of life, and inspired, full of God's Spirit, then we are not really dependent in the negative sense, but are truly free. If we are dependent on that which is vital and inspired, we will be free of morbid dependencies. Vital and inspired dependencies include first our loving Creator, then our families, church, and civic organizations. Our schools were once vital and inspired places of learning before becoming modernist seminaries of humanism, and they can be again.

Thrift and Prudence

Thrift and *prudence*—old-fashioned words that may seem quaint in our jaded culture. However, they are essential virtues for the survival and prosperity of a nation. They are essential virtues for a family, a state, and a nation. If we are sincere about leaving this world a better place for the next generation, then we need to turn over to them a nation that is debt-free.

Thrift is simply the "quality of using money and other resources carefully and not wastefully." *Prudence* means "acting with and showing thought for the future."

The simple antidote to our ruinous debt problem is simple: to sincerely pursue fiscal policy that exercises thrift and prudence. We need not despair. This is not complicated. The answer is right in front of us. It always has been and it will never change. We simply need to accept the truth, reach for the solutions, and ask for God's help.

Blossoming

In this cultural conditions report, I have searched for a word that best describes the opposite of decadence. *Blossoming* may seem like an odd word choice, but if you look at all the rancor, discord, and dispiriting behavior around us, blossoming is the last thing you would think of to honestly describe our culture. An image of what we have lost through deleterious decadence could be a dried and withered bouquet. The opposite of this is a thriving, robust, blossoming rose garden. There could be an almost endless list of decadent behaviors and choices. There is just as long a list of virtuous choices and behaviors that will cause us to blossom as a people and as a culture. It is not too hard to come up with an image in our minds of individuals or families building their lives around several core virtues: Honesty, sincerity, trust, gentleness, compassion (real), generosity. It is easy to visualize individuals and families that truly embody these characteristics blossoming and growing, developing into people of character that are the true givers around us. The same choices are before all of us individually and collectively: to reject or accept, to wither and die or blossom and bloom.

We have never been a perfect people. There was never any time in our past that was without some of the negative characteristics we see in our culture now. We cannot return to some nostalgic vision of our past, but we can resolve to reverse the downward cycle. Moving forward with wisdom, faith, hope and charity will save the day.

"I . . . call upon America to be more careful with its trust. . . . Prevent those . . . from falsely using social justice to lead you down a false road. They are trying to weaken you. We can only reach for the warm hand of God, which we have so rashly and self-confidently pushed away."
ALEKSANDR SOLZHENITSYN

FOUR
DENIAL-A CONVENIENT DECEPTION

"We have been blind, and in our blindness our enemy has returned."
GANDALF, THE HOBBIT, J.R.R. TOLKIEN

*"In our country the lie has become not just
a moral category but a pillar of the state."*
ALEKSANDR SOLZHENITSYN

"BIKE MAINE" IS a weeklong organized bicycling expedition through the state of Maine. I usually sign up for several of these types of trips during any given year. This particular ride has about 350 riders. It involves a kind of communal living as we move from town to town. Meals are shared, and there are ample opportunities to make new friends along the way. At breakfast one day, I was seated across from a retired CIA agent. I asked him if there was anything he had worked on that he was free to discuss. He told me he had been involved in preparing reports on the weaknesses of the Soviet Union toward the end of the Cold War. He was a bit defensive since the CIA completely misjudged how weak the Soviet Union was and didn't foresee the collapse, and he added that they were only charged with looking at military, not economic, weaknesses. I asked him what a foreign country would say about the United States if they were preparing such a report. What weaknesses would our enemies see if they took an empirical look at all aspects of our society?

As an example I asked about our federal debt. Shouldn't we be losing sleep over this massive, unsustainable debt? He told me it was really only a small percentage of the national GDP and not something I should be overly concerned about. He compared it to a family making $400,000 a year and having $20,000 in credit card debt. As I reflected on this later, I realized it was a completely flawed analogy. We should not look at the federal debt as a percentage of the GDP—we should look at it as a percentage of the federal budget.

I caught up with my friend later in the day and challenged his analogy. We shouldn't look at the debt as a percentage of the GDP because it's not their money. The correct analogy is that our government is like a family making $100,000 a year with $700,000 in non-collateral credit card debt. This family spends 30 percent of their household budget just making interest payments on non-collateral debt. Such a family—like our country—is *crippled* by debt. Thirty percent of the family's paycheck is not going toward investments such as a house or car. Thirty percent of their paycheck is not being spent on food or clothing. It can't be put into college savings. For a government, 30 percent of the taxes they collect can't be spent on roads, universities, or basic government services. It is as if 30 percent of the budget is being stolen every year. The amount of the debt service is close to the amount that the federal government borrows. Therefore we are borrowing and adding more debt just to make interest payments and service the debt! We are increasing the debt just to make interest payments on the existing debt. In aeronautics, this is called a death spiral.

My friend finally conceded that this is a huge problem though his only solution is more taxes. An obviously very intelligent, caring, and sincere man, he just seems to have been steeped for many years in the culture of denial that is prevalent in our nation's capital.

What other critical weaknesses would someone on the outside looking in see in the financial, and social state of our country that we ourselves deny and are blind to? What is the true state of our economic, governmental, and societal systems?

Denial, another word for *pride*, is at the heart of almost all personal and societal problems. If we cannot honestly admit what our real problems are, and their severity, there is no real hope of getting on a path to recovery. If we find the humility to admit our faults and failings, at this point in history, then solutions will flow to us naturally. We will find ourselves in possession of new reserves of power and direction.

Modernism asserts certain fundamental beliefs or denials. Primarily and above all, it denies the existence of a sovereign God, a God who is our Creator and Maker. We've forgotten that how we believe we came to exist, no matter the time line, has a great deal of impact on our daily lives. If there is no sovereign God, then there are also no immutable truths of human nature. There is no spiritual order to the universe and no governing principles we are to live by. There is no divine guidance, only the dictates of flawed human nature.

The idea that we are all faulty and fallen creatures has been rejected by modernists. As fallen creatures, many of us welcomed these ideas. To reject God and live by our own will and wits is what most of us are naturally inclined to do, while rejecting our own wills and seeking divine direction requires work, conviction, and supernatural inspiration.

Without a God, there are no absolute principles to live by. Without divine precepts to live by, we no longer govern our own behaviors. This leads to moral anarchy, which leads to social chaos. To control this, the government then begins to micromanage every aspect of our lives. There is then a downward cycle of less and less restraint by individuals and groups that is always followed by more and more control by government.

With God there is clear guidance for our lives. Following these divine precepts, we no longer want or need every aspect of our lives to be governed and subsidized. We can do the right things without the need for "governing legal authority." We then have something of real freedom. Vital dependence on our loving Creator displaces morbid dependence on a human government. For obvious reasons this would be very unsettling for those that are in the denial and dependence industries that drive most of our media and government today.

Or perhaps modernist leaders *are* very aware of human nature. Perhaps they know it is easier to tempt us to abdicate responsibility for our lives than to have the courage and conviction to lead us—by actions and example—to higher things. They simply aren't constrained by a God-directed conscience. And if we are honest, most of us might admit that we would rather have our self-centered behavior excused and justified than be confronted about it. True love, caring, and compassion confront and challenge us to better things. They are *honest*.

Modernism operates in an insulated world where the only voices are those that support their delusions. Those that don't agree with them are characterized as being on the lunatic fringe. They never imagine that they themselves are the lunatics. They are startled when they hear the truth presented in a clear, honest, and sincere manner.

It is characteristic of those that are in denial, individually or collectively, that they react violently when presented with the truth of their situation. This may be physical violence, but more often the attacks are against the character of those that are bringing some light to the situation. Those in denial spend tremendous energy and are incredibly cunning in convincing others that those shining the light of truth are in fact the ones with the problem.

In politics and media those in denial will almost always have the same two reactions to having the light of truth shone on their actions. They will "muddy the waters" by attempting to confuse and redirect the conversation or they will "shoot the messenger."

Every year the American Institute of Architects (AIA) hosts a national convention. There my fellow architects and I attend a variety of seminars in order to obtain our required continuing education credits. Topics are diverse across the spectrum of the many areas of study and specialization in architecture. Some topics are loftier, covering design philosophy and historic preservation. Others are more prosaic, informing us of building code updates and liability protection.

At one of these annual conventions, I signed up for a seminar on revitalizing urban neighborhoods. I've spent a lot of time working, volunteering, and investing in the inner city, and I hoped to gain some practical information to apply to developing and "revitalizing" properties back home in Trenton, New Jersey. The speakers were mostly representatives from the Department of Housing and Urban Development or architects in private practice that work with them. The AIA is a decidedly an "inside the Beltway" type of organization, and conventions tend to have a politically correct atmosphere. I quickly realized that this particular seminar was going to be overtly partisan and political. Ad hominem attacks on some political leaders and endorsement of others were tossed out before there was any talk of housing.

Independent professionals accept that most past models for planned and subsidized urban developments have failed. But the presenters of this seminar believed that the model for urban housing renewal over the past sixty years had not been wrong, but simply underfunded. Their urban planning solutions did not present anything new, nothing creative or original. Surprisingly the presenters did not question the paradigm at all; there was no discussion about what may have been successful or what had failed historically. There was no talk of how organic, spontaneous improvements have come about without government intervention. They dismissed the many failed housing projects that have been abandoned, shut down, or completely demolished by demonizing leadership in the opposing political party.

Many traditional, planned urban housing projects have been a failure. Design professionals have learned that social problems can't be solved with buildings. As much as architects would like to solve these problems with our buildings, we realize that we can't change a community by only changing building structures. The problems are not that superficial. Creating what are supposed to be clean and orderly engineered environments and expecting people to live accordingly doesn't work.

It is not that the buildings themselves were faulty and had to be condemned. They were built at great cost with substantial construction systems that were intended to last a hundred years. The unsettling thing that we don't want to admit is that the buildings became uninhabitable because of the abuse and neglect of the residents.

But as the presenters of this seminar demonstrated, *denial* is rampant. Denial of the root causes of the problems; denial that the approach and subsequent projects failed; denial of human nature, denial of their own culpability. Denial is at the root of most of life's problems. People make wrong choices and begin to experience the consequences. Rather than look at themselves, they shift the blame. It is someone else's fault, or their circumstances are to blame. Some people will find a caretaker. On a personal level this may be a parent, spouse, or other individual. In society this might be a politician—a modernist leader.

In the cacophony of public discourse, it helps to gain clarity if we look at things on a personal level. Just as furniture is "small architecture," the individual is the microcosm of the larger human organization. Take an adult male who struggles with finances, relationships, or addiction. This person can no longer manage his life. He may have had problems in the past that he had no control over. Perhaps he was the victim of violence or oppression. Or maybe he has gone through the same trials the rest of us do but has made it bigger than it was, and it has become the excuse for his current problems. For whatever reason this person has been unable to move on.

Unwilling to deal with the past in an honest and spiritually mature way, he starts to surround himself with more and more like-minded people. In what we call democracy, eventually this group can then become a voting bloc. They find a leader that tells them what they want to hear. "It's not your fault, others are to blame. You need— *you have a right to*—financial assistance and compensation for past wrongs."

What if other communities or groups that up to this point had been self-sufficient see this and start to get resentful and envious of this first group that appears to be getting something for nothing? Envy becomes greed. "We want some of that too!" So that community's leader gets together with the first to work out a scheme to satisfy both. Then another community, and another community or group join in, until there are more and more feeding at the public trough and fewer and fewer to fill it.

I have a little more faith in people than that. I don't think most communities would start clamoring for remuneration from the public trust entirely on their own. I have spoken to people who grew up dirt poor. They told me that growing up without even shoes to wear, they didn't think of themselves as poor. They spoke of being happy, joyous, and free. They didn't spend their days being envious or bitter about their circumstances until someone—a politician, an activist—told them they should be.

There are those also that are not wholly dependent on handouts from the citizen's treasury but are a burden just the same. The unions and workers' groups that are dependent on forced government intervention. They are dependent on "make work" projects to maintain employment levels while the rest of us experience belt tightening. They are dependent on government to maintain what may be oversized salaries and benefits. Their salaries actually go up during times of hardship, while unprotected citizen workers have to make cuts. They are oversized if that group is receiving well beyond what their level of education and degree of service would be worth in a free economy. We speak mostly of the welfare state, but there is now an almost *endless* list of dependents, from farmers to Wall Street investors and huge banking empires.

Most often the protests over this modernist governance is over redistributing earned income to those who have not earned it. *The real tragedy is what it does to the hearts, minds, and souls of all involved.* The providers cease to be real leaders. There are no longer statesmen, only politicians. For the recipients, all the will and spirit goes out of them as they give up on themselves. For those footing the bill, there is the discouragement of knowing their hard-earned income is being sent to those who haven't earned it and to their lobbyists, paid from the same taxes, arguing for even higher taxes.

There are those that are truly unable to care for themselves. They should be given all the kindness, mercy, and care we can provide. But when a large, centralized government tries to do this, there are infinite opportunities for corruption on the part of givers and receivers who aren't truly in need.

The only way I have seen people recover from such circumstances is by the application of timeless spiritual truths; this enables them to see things in a new light. What if, rather than developing a community of dependents, they sought to develop a community of independents and interdependents—or better still, a community that seeks to give more than it takes?

Bringing the discussion back to a personal level again, if a person deals with his or her emotional pain and life problems as they arise, life goes on and balance returns. When problems aren't faced and dealt with, they mount. When a person chooses food, drugs, or adultery to avoid the pain, the original problem never goes away, and what started as a diversion becomes an even bigger problem in and of itself.

God will always provide the wherewithal to meet our needs and deal with challenges as they arise. I don't think He's willing to foot the bill for the excesses, though. So we beg, steal, and borrow from the future to pay for today's gratification.

Just as an individual can stop dealing with life's problems and start relying on false solutions, so can a society. No person or society travels a straight path to success and fullness of purpose. But when a crisis or temporary downturn becomes a long-term problem, if an individual or a society refuses to face the truth of a situation, the real source of trouble is *denied*, and the problem is compounded.

What works for an individual works for a family, a town, a city, and a nation. If a nation squarely faces its problems as they arise, balance is restored. If a less courageous attempt at a solution is made or the temptation to exploit the situation is not resisted, then problems persist and grow. The principles that ensure a joyous, happy, and free life for an individual are no different from what works for any institution or nation.

Modernism is a spiritually sick system, and at the heart of any sick system is denial. Modernists deny the destructiveness of their beliefs and actions; they deny the truth about human nature that make their social engineering solutions unworkable failures. They deny that their current movement, no matter what they label it, shares the same ideological roots as other recent modernist movements that have caused most of the death and destruction of the past one hundred years.

Those who fall into addictions stop addressing their inner and outer pain and problems and replace solutions and resolutions with denials and a drink. The problem doesn't go away. They are always deferring payment until it mounts up and the day of crisis comes. In a similar way modernist societies expand their dependence on centralized government that supposedly will solve their every woe. The power-hungry are all too happy to assume more power. The spiritually and emotionally unhealthy are willing to give control of their lives over to someone who promises to take care of them. Social and economic problems are never really solved. The blame is merely shifted; the new program is created and funded. Someone is demonized as the creator of the problem; there is scapegoating and mob justice. A new self-perpetuating industry is created whose grist is bitterness, self-righteousness, and self-pity. The end product is dispiriting and demoralizing for all involved. A culture moving toward modernism is a culture in a cycle of decay and decline.

The early modernists were blunter in their reforms or revolutions. They told us they would free us from the corruption they saw amongst the religious and the greed of the robber barons and deliver us to a utopia of freedom, equality, and brotherhood. Ignoring the realities of human nature, modernists have unleashed more death and destruction than any other ideology or natural catastrophe in history.

There was a movement that started among the most intellectual elites of one European culture in the early twentieth century that eventually become the cause of the most brutish, ignorant, and hateful treatment of another culture. This culture embraced all the primary tenants of modernism. They had a socialist economy. Their ideology was driven by Social Darwinism. They demonized traditional and orthodox religion. All ideas that are dominant in our culture now. Their cause célèbre was a man-designed human race: eugenics. Its adherents included the founder of our primary "family planning" organization. What became their greatest atrocity started with a plan to eliminate the mentally and physically deformed from the gene pool. "Euthanizing" the institutionalized with mental illnesses and the physically disfigured. It became the Holocaust.

Denying the realities of fallen human nature is the crux of it all. Modernists propose textbook solutions to problems that deny the effects of greed for power and control, bigotry, sloth, and the other host of defects that beset us all.

Modernists have tried to reengineer our sexual identities, our families, our cities, and our love relationships, and they have reengineered our government, but their science has been fatally flawed. New philosophies of freedom and fulfillment in our sex lives brings epidemics of disease and millions of broken hearts. They think that they can change the way that we think about ourselves as men and women, how we love and teach our children. Real science would be empirical and would recognize the negative returns of modernism. It would accept the *truths* about our human condition.

Being in a state of denial will always produce unhealthy, morbid dependencies. Humility, honesty, and truth will always result in vital and healthy dependencies and interdependence.

Our culture and our media are constantly inundating us with the same emotional attacks that modernists have been prosecuting for over a hundred years. There are constant attacks on religion, free economies, and traditional institutions, as if they present some great threat to humanity. The modernist movement is what we should be driving from our culture and guarding ourselves and our children against. This is the "real and present danger." We will start solving our problems when we start admitting this *truth*.

We have been blind, and in our blindness the enemies of slavish and dispiriting dependencies, ruinous debt, and deleterious decadence have returned.

Reading the headlines every day, it is very easy to become discouraged, but we need not be. There are very simple spiritual truths that, if followed, will heal us as a people. So if you will, it begins with this first step: to simply and honestly admit our true faults and failings at this time in history.

The fruit of acknowledging the truth is a new freedom and a spiritual energy that will propel us forward. We will feel like that giant hand has grabbed us by the back of our shirt collar, lifted us up, and propelled us in the right direction. We need God's help, His truth, His power, and His guidance. Turning to His timeless precepts will lead to being happy, joyous, and free to serve others.

"For here we can follow truth wherever it may lead."
THOMAS JEFFERSON

FIVE

COUNTERFEIT COMPASSION

"Every evil screams only one message: 'I am good.'"
ALEXANDER SCHMEMANN

OLD BUILDINGS TALK to me. Of course, you don't have to be an architect for buildings to talk to you, but it provides more insight.

I love old things. When I was a child, I loved old items that told me about another person in another time. Holding a 400-year-old Native American stone axe head in my hands, I would think about the life of the one who fashioned and wielded it. I would imagine what their life was like—the simplicity, the hardship, the danger. I also think how impossible it would be for them to imagine the culture, life, and person of someone that would hold their work hundreds of years later.

Working with old buildings is similar, but on a larger scale.

Red Bank, New Jersey

One of my projects was a Baptist church in Red Bank, New Jersey. It was a Romanesque structure made of glazed, iron spot, Roman-style brick and a slate roof. The moldings were painted wood, with a tower cornice of painted, galvanized sheet metal. I was told that it had been designed by the same architect who designed Carnegie Hall.

This church had been "restored" ten years prior to my service there. The previous restoration contractors did little more than cover up the significant problems the building had. Churches are easy prey for unscrupulous restoration contractors. The badly rusted sheet metal cornice on the tower was caulked, patched, and covered with a heavy coat of paint to give the appearance of restoration. When my team began to investigate closely, the metal came apart in our hands. Reaching into the cornice and pulling out a handful of debris and nesting material, I found a .22 caliber lead bullet. The church was in a downtown area, not in a field or in the woods. This caused me to wonder how this projectile got there.

Red Bank is close to where I grew up, so I am somewhat familiar with the area and its history. My father grew up around the corner from this church on Reckless Place, a street name that has always disturbed me. Not that a street name determines how someone's life turns out, but it bothers me just the same. Red Bank still looks like a Hardy Boys' neighborhood, with the character of pre-World War II housing, something lacking in almost all housing built after the war.

I can only speculate on why someone would be taking shots at the bell tower of this church sixty, eighty, or a hundred years ago. Perhaps someone was taking shots at pigeons on the roof, or perhaps it was a prank that would have not been taken too seriously at the time. One can only speculate; however, there was a time not too long ago when life was so simple and safe in this downtown neighborhood that someone could take a potshot at pigeons on the roof without much of a response other than shouts from angry neighbors. There was a time not too many decades back when a young man could walk down the streets of our Eastern towns with a rifle under his arm, on his way to the woods or the river, and not cause a stir. *There was a time when we weren't so afraid of our youth or each other.*

There was a time when most every family was not somehow so tragically affected by the cultural changes around us.

Spring Lake, New Jersey

St. Catharine's Church is located in the affluent town of Spring Lake, New Jersey. Spring Lake used to be referred to as the "Irish Riviera" because of its oceanfront location and the fact that it was mostly populated by wealthy Irish Catholic families. The church was built in 1900 and funded by one man, Martin Maloney, a successful Philadelphia businessman and philanthropist. He donated it to the Diocese of Trenton, New Jersey, and dedicated it to the memory of his sixteen-year-old daughter, Catherine

"Kitty" Maloney, who had died from tuberculosis while traveling to Europe for treatment.

As the architect for the restoration of this edifice, I had access to every nook and cranny of this building. In the attic I found a small copper candleholder fashioned from a scrap of copper used on the roof. On a cornice, inside the nave, I found a craft paper "cartoon" used by an artist to map out a portrait in a mural. I thought about these two craftsmen whose hands were stilled long ago: ordinary men creating beautiful things, not thinking overly much of themselves for doing it. So different from our times when many think too highly of themselves and believe they are entitled to too much for doing little or nothing at all!

The outside of the building had been fully covered in scaffolding so we could replace the copper sheathing on the hundred-year-old dome and restore the masonry. At the very top of the cupola, I found a large caliber bullet hole that entered and exited near the top of the cross. I knew it had been here for a long time, since the jagged edges of the exit hole had been worn smooth over the years by the feet of seagulls and pigeons. The angle of the entrance and exit holes indicate that the shooter was right in front of the church and used a .30-06 caliber or larger rifle. Some old timers seemed to think they knew who it was; it must have been someone who was a pretty good shot.

Other Places

Once, while renovating a large home on the Navesink River, I found a space the size of a closet that was sealed on all sides with three layers of plaster and metal lath. The only item in this space was a metal box containing letters between the doctor that lived there in the 1800s and his mistress who lived in New York City. The last correspondence was a letter from the mistress threatening suicide. What interesting discoveries we make when we start going over every inch of these old structures!

What I love about old buildings and artifacts is that they connect me to the essence and character of another era. Although there have been no perfect or idyllic times in our history, we can take the best from the past and cherish it. This gives us inspiration and ideals to strive for. As our first president said, they allow us "to raise up a standard that those who choose may repair to."

My work has brought me often to the neighborhoods not so affluent and quiet as Spring Lake or Red Bank. Much of my work with churches brings me to the inner cities of New York, New Jersey, and Pennsylvania. As I drive through the rundown neighborhoods, these buildings talk to me too. They tell me stories of another kind, stories that make me grieve. What were once grand, single-family homes are still there, but they have lost all their luster. Under the aluminum cladding, the many layers of gray and brown, the purple paint and deteriorated masonry, they tell me that these used to be special places that were alive and thriving. Places where you could take in the advent of spring on your front porch or enjoy a quiet summer evening, with the thought of sudden danger the furthest thing from your mind. Now sudden danger and calamity might come unannounced at any moment of the day or night.

I was called to a church in Camden for a possible restoration and renovation project. I pulled up and saw evidence of someone taking shots at a church again. This time it was semi-automatic gunfire sprayed through the large stained glass window—not an innocent prank.

I have shopped for investment properties in Trenton, New Jersey. It's been a good place for me to invest, but the enduring charm of the houses draws me to the area as well.

West State Street was the grand avenue of Trenton, and to some extent it still is, depending on the block. Once the most successful and affluent doctors, lawyers, politicians, and businessmen built homes here, before the "great white flight" from urban areas. These grand old mansions testify to the large, multigenerational families that once thrived here. A few blocks over are the working-class neighborhoods that were once a vehicle to bigger and better things but are now testaments to generational poverty, anger, and despair.

As a historic architect, I gain access to places in old buildings others don't get to see. First Baptist Peddie Memorial Church in Newark features a Byzantine-style dome and Romanesque towers and arcades. Designed by William Halsey Wood in the nineteenth century, it was completed in 1888 and is listed on the National Register of Historic Places. Vitruvius, the famous Roman architect, wrote about the three elements of good architecture: firmness, commodity, and delight. This church is magnificent and delightful. The sanctuary boasts a grand circular plan with vaulted bead board ceilings. The interior front of the church reveals remote sitting alcoves, single balconies, and a small private, paneled library as one ascends the steps to the bell tower. The interior is badly deteriorated, the sad evidence of an urban church that cannot meet the demands of maintaining an old building with limited resources.

It grieves me to see these structures in such a sad state. It grieves me far more to see the strife and danger that are part of everyday life here now. Like the buildings, the people have lost their spirit and their sense of purpose. There is no momentum, no moving forward, and little hope.

The reasons for this are not what we want to hear and not what we want to say. We don't want to say that the responsibility for the decline of these areas rests with those that live here. We don't know how to articulate that the fault lies with those that claim to be the saviors of the inner city. Haven't we been stubborn and ignorant in insisting that all that is needed is ever larger infusions of cash and new government programs?

The inner cities have been the primary laboratories for modernism. Untold billions of dollars have been poured into them in hopes of finding humanist solutions to the problems. Because the solutions have been based on flawed, shallow human "wisdom," they have failed catastrophically, and the results are utter devastation. An invading army could not have done more damage. At least an invading army would have left the spirit of the people intact. The modernists with their failed ideology and fraudulent propaganda have stripped all that they can of what makes for a good life in a good community. There is a near mathematical correlation between morbid government expansion and the decline of vital institutions.

My own experience is not unlike that of many of those who live in the inner cities. At one time, I suffered abuse and misfortune that I did not deserve. I was dispirited and without hope. The circumstances that brought me to that point were out of my control, and for a while I abdicated responsibility for my own life and blamed circumstances for my problems. I was filled with self-pity, bitterness, resentment, and an overwhelming sense of entitlement. In such a state there wasn't much anyone could do for me until I accepted that the solution to my plight required me to let go of my excuses and stop blaming others.

The defects or lack of character that serve to bring an individual down also will bring a group of people down. If one abdicates responsibility for oneself and is dominated by self-pity, envy, and entitlement, one will become ensnared by those beliefs and will not be happy, productive, or free. In the same way, a community or even a nation dominated by these destructive convictions will not prosper or be free. On the flip side, the same attributes that will bring joy and freedom to an individual will do the same for a community, a state, or a nation.

One has to ask if modernism is inherently racist. Its proponents certainly have been successful in appealing to the moral vanity of the affluent in promoting their worldview, while the poor and the minorities have been buried by their revolution.

True Compassion, Tough Love

True compassion, by its very nature, does not bring enumeration of any kind to the giver other than the joy of selfless giving. False compassion brings power and material wealth to those that bestow it. Real compassion carries with it wisdom and honesty. It gives freely and generously but also has a tough love that speaks courageously and honestly. Counterfeit compassion would rather not risk rejection, by speaking the truth in love, but instead hides the truth in order to garner as many votes and as much power as possible.

True compassion has the capacity to lift up and liberate the recipient, while false compassion only serves to dispirit and emasculate the recipient by maintaining a downward cycle of abdication of responsibility, more control by others, and loss of liberty and self-respect.

What doesn't work for an individual will not work for a village, a city, a state, or a nation. A life lived in bitterness and self-pity, expecting others to pay one's way, is a failed life. Governance by the same flawed or defective motives, no matter how effective and enticing the propaganda, is just as much of a failure.

Those that truly helped me out of my circumstances did not coddle me or listen to my excuses. They confronted me about my delusional and dishonest thinking. They did not set themselves up to be gods in my life, but instead directed me to the true God.

If we honestly acknowledge how corrupt and perverted the current notion of compassion, administered through government, has become we can begin to act with real and true compassion. Lives will be lifted up rather than brought down if we act with honesty, wisdom, and true charity.

As William J. H. Boetcker said:

> You cannot bring about prosperity by discouraging thrift.
> You cannot strengthen the weak by weakening the strong.
> You cannot help little men by tearing down big men.
> You cannot lift the wage earner by pulling down the wage payer.
> You cannot help the poor by destroying the rich.
> You cannot establish sound security on borrowed money.
> You cannot further the brotherhood of man by inciting class hatred.
> You cannot keep out of trouble by spending more than you earn.
> You cannot build character and courage by destroying men's initiative and independence.[1]

And you cannot help men permanently by doing for them what they can and should do for themselves.

"It is time in the West to defend not so much human rights
as human obligations."
ALEKSANDR SOLZHENITSYN

---

1 William J. H. Boetcker, *The Ten Cannots* (leaflet). This quote has often been falsely attributed to Abraham Lincoln. See https://en.wikipedia.org/wiki/William_J._H._Boetcker.

SIX

MODERN GODS-AMERICAN IDOLS

*"Our hearts were made for You, O Lord,
and they are restless until they rest in you."*
St. Augustine

HIGHWAY 195 CUTS across New Jersey at the center of the state from east to west and leads to Trenton, the state capitol. I'm often on this road in the morning on my way to a work meeting or to tend to a problem at a rental property. Much of this rush-hour traffic consists of state agency workers, bureaucrats off to spend their day making life a bit more difficult than necessary for the rest of us. One morning a compact car passed me with a bumper sticker that read, "Nature is God." I'm pretty sure the driver was on his or her way to a job at the Department of Environmental Protection.

Phillipsburg Alliance Church is a vibrant, vital, growing church in North Jersey across the Delaware River from Easton, Pennsylvania. This has always been a blue-collar, working-class area. Originally developed for the local manufacturing and mining economy, now the residents mostly commute to New York City. It's at the far end of the commuting lines, and therefore living costs are lower. People are willing to commute over two hours to the city in order to enjoy a simpler, more rural lifestyle. Hard-earned money goes into the collection plate each Sunday.

The church began as a one-story building that formerly housed a hardware store. Outgrowing this building, the church leaders contacted my firm to design an addition. The plan was to add a second story with a 250-seat sanctuary. The unsound front section had to be taken down and replaced with a two-story narthex. To minimize the feeling of having to climb to the second-floor worship area, we designed a wide L-shaped stairway with a gentle rise. At the landing we installed a large circular window looking toward the western horizon. For the most part all the work was done without incurring debt. Walls were raised and the roof put on as funds came in or work and materials were donated. Progress was slow, but over the span of a few years, we were able to complete the project, and the church moved into their new sanctuary debt-free. The growing congregation quickly started to outgrow their new addition, and they started to look for a site to build a larger church home.

In New Jersey, it's a very difficult process for a church to find a piece of land to build a new church. Typically the zoned minimum lot size for a new church is nine acres or more. The parcels of land that would be suitable for a church to build on are also attractive to developers and therefore expensive. The economy of the past few years has helped bring down real estate prices to a more affordable level, but it is still challenging. Add to this the arduous process of obtaining zoning, engineering, and environmental approvals, and the process can take years before breaking ground.

Over the years the church approached the local planning board with tracts of land they were interested in purchasing. They were declined several times before they found a piece of land that was available, affordable, and met the approval of the township and other agencies. The church felt this was going to be the perfect location for their new building complex. They started the zoning approval process and did all their homework before closing on the property to make sure they would be able to get all necessary engineering and environmental approvals. The town had already given them preliminary approval.

Weeks after closing on this property, the then-governor of New Jersey needed a distraction from his political problems. He had recently been exposed for appointing his gay lover to a critical government security position that he had no experience for. Added to that were charges of arranging approvals to politically connected and corrupt developers. Developers with more cash and less scruples than those hired by the church were able to have the skids greased for an expedited approval process.

The Highlands Water Resource Preservation Act, a piece of legislation that had languished on the back burner for decades, was rushed forward for the governor's signature and photo opportunity. This act focused on an area of private land and made it impossible to build all but the most minor structures. Not only did it prohibit the land owners from starting future projects, it was retroactive to months before the signing of the legislation. A land owner could have spent hundreds of thousands of dollars on gaining approvals for a project, but if they didn't have 100 percent approval at the retroactive date, their project was dead. If one signature was missing, all their efforts were for naught. For the Phillipsburg Alliance Church, this meant that the usable area of their newly purchased thirty-acre tract was less than one acre.

The governor had his distraction. The environmental activists in the state capitol had what they wanted. But for the Phillipsburg Alliance Church, their project was dead, and they were left with a multimillion-dollar mortgage on a cornfield.

Ironically the church found relief in federal legislation signed into law by another scandal-plagued political leader—legislation that gives relief from overzealous government planners to religious and other non-profit organizations. To this end they have hired a Washington, D.C., law firm that specializes in such situations. I was invited to a meeting with the attorneys as they were discussing the players, the attorneys, and environmental officials that oppose them. Speaking of the appointed environmental officials and the opposition we faced, one attorney commented, *"You have to understand, this is their religion."* Two religions. One worshipping the Creator of the universe, the God of peace and reconciliation. Another religion revering created, material things. Maybe not so much giving religious meaning to creation, but religious zealotry to their cause. In this case at least, we have the worshipers of nature, with the power of the state, imposing their religion on another. Not so much prudent custodians of the environment around us as religious zealots.

This environmentalism is not based on science and empirical study but on a neo-pagan worship of created things. It reflects a new asceticism that seeks to find a religious experience through the preservation of a pure and perfect environment, with no regard for truly being good stewards and wise users of the natural gifts our Creator has given us.

In the disharmony and conflict created by the moral anarchy of modernism, reckless developers and environmentalists share the same mind-set: They are both materialists, placing their hopes for security in the material world.

When separated from real conservation and science, modernism can be a great hindrance to freedom and prosperity. When modernistic materialism and moral relativism permeate our financial world, they destroy the means of one's financial support in proportion to one's vulnerability.

We most often associate the threat of modernism with areas where its power is concentrated— the state level, the media, and academia. What happens when the principles of modernism secrete themselves into other institutions? What happens when materialism and moral relativism dominate the actions of those in control of our financial institutions? We are told that there are no absolutes. We are told there is no God—or at least no God we really need to be concerned with. We are told that we are the arbiters of our own conduct. No one should judge anyone else. Why are we then so shocked at the recklessness and greed that result when individuals act out the moral lessons they have been taught in school and through media outlets?

When we unleash the lesser angels of our nature by every man, woman, and child choosing to be their own gods, there can never be enough programs, laws, regulations, jails, or mental institutions to contain the fallout.

Human nature is inclined toward selfishness. Look at any day care center play area, and you'll observe this. "Mine, mine, mine!" Selflessness and virtue require work. Virtue requires putting aside our own skewed, relativistic ideas of right and wrong and looking to higher ideals not established by our own flawed natures. Virtue involves pushing the wheelbarrow up the hill. Vice, on the other hand, hops in and zooms down the hill, not realizing there are no brakes and the only way to stop is to crash.

Modernist leaders are infinitely creative and seductive in finding ways to sell vice as virtue, selfishness as selflessness. In the most deceptive ways, they play to our fears and greatest moral flaws. They espouse their way as the compassionate way. However, there is a very simple way to test the purity of a leader's prognostications. In the long run, do these philosophies result in more power and control for them and less for us? True charity does not build up its own power base in the process.

In this type of moral anarchy, the only man that is not accepted is the man that says not everything is acceptable. The modernists during the Cold War era told us they didn't love Communism—they just hated those who hated Communism. In a similar way, modernists lead themselves and others to believe that they don't love sin—they just hate those that hate sin. They don't hate God; they just hate those that love Him and His ways.

There are many different denominations of modernism and many different labels—Communism, socialism, liberalism, progressivism, humanism, secularism, National Socialism—but they all share the same core beliefs:

- We are soulless, evolved beings. We are not brought into this world by a Creator, nor are we accountable to Him.

- There are no established, timeless laws of human nature or precepts established by a Creator that work for our benefit or detriment if we do or don't adhere to them. Man's wisdom is the supreme authority.

The truth is that we are created and fallen creatures with a need to worship. If we aren't worshiping the true God, we'll worship one of the counterfeit gods of nature, materialism, or other created beings. This includes worshiping men and the "wisdom" of man.

Hindsight is always 20/20, but it is much more difficult to see clearly what is truly going on in current events. We can look at Germany eighty years ago and recognize the horrible evil that took place there. How many of us could have recognized it if we were there when it was developing? After all, Germany was prospering when the rest of the world was stuck in the Depression. They were at the forefront of progressive, humanist ideology promoting peace and prosperity for all. The holocaust began as a eugenics movement concerned with the quality of life for the deformed, the handicapped, and the mentally ill. It started with euthanizing children with cleft palates—it was the compassionate thing to do; they were suffering. Their "quality of life" was not what it should be.

We look now at backwoods militia camps and all the undereducated followers with shaved heads and swastikas, and of course we condemn Nazism as ignorant and brutish. But the National Socialist Workers

Party wasn't started by the ignorant and brutish. What became the Holocaust was started by doctors, lawyers, and philosophers. It began with Social Darwinists who wanted to engineer a new society, rooting out what the founder of our own family planning movement, Margaret Sanger, called "human weeds." [2] We can look at the crude representatives of this ideology and decry it, but can we get past our denial and see that there are shared legacies in our own culture now? In addition to being obsessed with overturning sexual mores, Sanger was above all a Malthusian eugenicist. Abortion and "family planning" clinics are typically located in the poorest minority neighborhoods. Why are the dear people of these neighborhoods targeted this way? Could it be a continuation of the same modernist eugenic belief system?

The great fatal flaw in modernism is that it denies the truths about human nature and tries to recreate man through "social engineering." Most of the founders of Germany's holocaust didn't set out to kill millions of people. They were seeking what they thought would be a better world, a reengineered human race. In the process they completely set aside any notion of deferring to the will of a Divine Creator. They no longer saw humanity as all created in God's image, precious in His sight. They had the power over right and wrong, life and death. They left out of their equations the realities of corrupt human nature and the universal human capacity for selfishness and hatred. An elitist formula for a new utopia thus became a hell on earth. Lacking humility and ignoring the truths of human nature, modernists set in motion their social plans that sound so benevolent but come back to us as a juggernaut.

Modernism always sounds very high-minded when advocating for one of their causes, such as quality of life and death with dignity. "Who is anyone else to say when a person can or can't choose to end their life?" they ask. After all the emotional arguments, shaming of opponents, activism and successful legislation, this can quickly become junior looking at Grandma sitting in front of a TV all day, her monthly care and medical bills quickly eroding that nice inheritance. Yes, it's time for them to start talking about doing the "right thing." Choice quickly

---

2 George Grant, *Grand Illusions: The Legacy of Planned Parenthood* (Nashville, TN: Wolgemuth & Hyatt, Publishers, Inc., 1988).

becomes coercion. What happens when "death with dignity" becomes the guiding principle of a bankrupt government that has taken over the healthcare system?

Worshiping Man

I consider the modernist's worship of man to be the most destructive ideology or belief in history.

> The crowds were so dense and chaotic outside that some people were trampled underfoot, others rammed against traffic lights, and some others choked to death. It is estimated that 500 people lost their lives while trying to get a glimpse of Stalin's corpse. Stalin had been a dictator and a tyrant. Yet he presented himself as the Father of Peoples, a wise leader, and the continuer of Lenin's cause. After his death, people began to acknowledge that he was responsible for the deaths of millions of their own countrymen. [3]

I suppose you could call Stalin the "pope" of modernism in his time. He was venerated in his country and by many in ours as well. While he was murdering millions of his own countrymen, the journalists of our most notable papers were singing his praises. Though they have painted themselves as victims, there were those in Hollywood that supported his murderous regime as well.

There have been many modernist man-gods in the past one hundred years. Stalin, Hitler, Mao, Castro, and Pol Pot to name a few of the most obvious and most destructive.

We have had our man-gods here in America. We may chafe at the thought, but looking at how some have responded to elections that haven't gone their way is telling. When modernists among us have had their leaders removed by elections and replaced with leaders that completely contradict their dogma, they react like religious zealots that have had their godhead removed. There is total hysteria and "much weeping and gnashing of teeth"; much "rending of their garments."

---

3 http://www.metafilter.com/33555/The-Posthumous-Peregrinations-of-Joseph-Stalin.

There is a difference between respecting and following leaders that protect our ability to pursue a life of freedom, prosperity, and happiness and a misplaced dependency on men or women to provide for us and be our security. If almost our whole sense of well-being is dependent on the man or woman at the podium, then we have replaced worshiping our Creator for revering a mere, flawed mortal.

In this modernist form of megalomania, the monuments man-gods create are their vast and all-encompassing programs. Roles are reversed: man is sovereign; God is subjugated. Man, projected through the eyes of a modernist, is omnipotent and omnipresent. God is passive and limited, a sentimental god. Man's dictates are absolute; God is relative. "What is truth"? asked Pontius Pilate. He and the modernist both scoff at the idea of absolutes.

Modernism's approach to true religion has been in turns overpowering, humiliating, dominating, crushing, dividing, intimidating, conquering, provoking, infiltrating, and seducing. At times modernism does sound very similar to the principles of Christianity, but it is darkness portraying itself as light. It is man counterfeiting the wisdom and virtue of God in a vain attempt to be like Him. On face value, it can look like the real article, and many believers have put the humanist principles of modernism ahead of orthodox Christianity. They might look similar, but they are diametrically opposed.

It's odd that the modernist sees man as a soulless creature evolved from primordial ooze and yet, at the same time, as the center of the cosmos, the center of the universe, and the top of the evolutionary pyramid. If not in words, at least in practice the modernist sees himself as the spearhead of evolution, but where does he get his direction? Not from a power above him. Not from the lessons of history. Only from his own small, corrupted intellect which has no power whatsoever to help guide him forward in a positive direction, separated as it is from the grace of God.

Modernism is man's self-will run amok on a global scale.

In confronting modernism, the faithful don't always present themselves very well. Sometimes they become caricatures of themselves. Sometimes their actions and billboards are simply crude and obnoxious, but just the same they are trying to point the way to a true God, the window to heaven.

If we can be honest about the state of spiritual sickness we are in, if we can admit we have replaced reverence for a real God with worship of flawed men and corrupt government and act with faith and love, then we can start to have something of real hope and recovery in all areas of our lives.

If we are to have peace and quiet in our culture, we have to stop playing God. In order to solve our manifold problems, we must allow our wills to be guided by the true benevolence of our loving Creator and follow His simple precepts and proverbial wisdom. Then we will be "happy and good."

We have no rest in our culture now, but we will have rest when we once again find rest in Him.

"The proper good of a creature is to surrender itself to its Creator—to enact intellectually, volitionally, and emotionally, that relationship which is given in the mere fact of its being a creature. When it does so, it is happy and good."
C. S. LEWIS

All men were by nature foolish who were in ignorance of God, and who from the good things seen did not succeed in knowing him who is, and from studying the works did not discern the artisan; But either fire, or wind, or the swift air, or the circuit of the stars, or the mighty water, or the luminaries of heaven, the governors of the world, they considered gods. Now if out of joy in their beauty they thought them gods, let them know how far more excellent is the Lord than these; for the original source of beauty fashioned them. Or if they were struck by their might and energy, let them from these things realize how much more powerful is he who made them.
THE BOOK OF WISDOM, CHAPTER 13

SEVEN

MAD MONEY—
PROSPERITY IS NOT A CRIME

*"There are two ways to conquer and enslave a country . . .
One is by the sword. The other is by debt."*
JOHN ADAMS

*"We don't even have a secretary of the treasury, we have a secretary
of the debt because there is no treasury, the treasury is empty,
and all we've got are liabilities . . ."*
PETER SCHIFF

THE QUADRANGLE AT Louisiana State University, where I attended college, is the center of campus. A rectangular courtyard about the size of a city block, it's filled with live oaks and surrounded by a Romanesque colonnade that allows students and staff to get from class to class while staying out of the frequent Louisiana downpours. It's bounded on three sides by the original campus buildings and on the fourth by the newer glass-and-concrete library. The glass-and-aluminum facade of the library is screened by Spanish moss-draped live oak trees. All the buildings have the same sand-colored cement plaster finish with an exposed aggregate of fine pea gravel. Rather than the rough texture of regular stucco, the small gravel makes it soft to the touch, worn smooth from the currents and tides of the rivers and beaches it came from. This finish is unique to the South and can be found everywhere in the buildings, amphitheaters, and sidewalks. It's a kinder, gentler concrete.

Back then, due to circumstances, I collected Social Security and Veterans benefits while enrolled in college. The memory that stays with me after so many years is the penetrating feeling that I was so deserving of this. It was a sense of entitlement born of being in a perpetual state of self-pity. As I walked that colonnade, flipped through my daily mail, and saw the desired envelope, a warm feeling rose up inside of me, a sense of getting something for nothing, a feeling of restitution for real or imagined wrongs. It was a sense that "Yes, the world *does* owe me a living"—a warm and satisfying feeling of having my self-pity validated.

Thoughts that perhaps someone else had worked for this money, that someone else may have been more deserving of it, did not occur to me at all. It seemed perfectly right and natural that because I had suffered, I should be somehow compensated. I didn't care about anyone else's plight; I was completely self-centered. Today there is a global epidemic of this kind of thinking.

A year earlier, while still enrolled at a local community college in New Jersey, I had managed to qualify for unemployment benefits from a job I had quit. Somehow I was able to convince the unemployment counselor that I had been laid off from this job instead. This was backed up with a call to my former department manager, an alcoholic. At the time, I was collecting Social Security, veteran's benefits, monies from a Basic Education Opportunity Grant, and, now I was illegally collecting unemployment benefits. I felt no embarrassment, no shame, and no pangs of guilt. In fact, I felt that I was simply entitled. It did prove to be a blessing in the long run, but thoughts of thanks and gratitude were far from me at age twenty. Besides, there wasn't anyone around to tell me otherwise. In fact, there were many—from the local bar stool to leaders in politics and media—that endorsed my position.

It is very hard to imagine a modernist leader suggesting that the recipients of such entitlements take some time to thank those that work to support them. What would happen if there was a block party thrown by a wholly subsidized neighborhood in honor of those that work to subsidize them? Or a moment of remembrance and gratitude at a state fair for all those that work to support farm subsidies? What about a national holiday to honor the 15 percent of taxpayers that carry most of the burden for the rest of us? It is indicative of how sick the system is that the idea of thanking the people and companies that bear most of the burden would be met with total outrage.

In New Jersey state funds for education are not apportioned equally. Affluent municipalities tend to spend about the median average per student, and almost all of those funds come from local property taxes. More impoverished townships can spend twice the average per student with less then 10 percent of those funds coming from local sources. Wouldn't it be appropriate for those lower income areas to have an attitude of gratitude for this advantage? It would be very refreshing and encouraging for those footing the bill to receive an occasional thank you. Much more important, it would benefit those receiving these gifts of additional funding. Having gratitude requires humility, and humility is an essential ingredient for a group or individual to be lifted up out of desperate situations.

Self-pity and self-justification come naturally to us. Persuading us with what comes naturally to our fallen human natures is not such hard work. Modernists deny that we have fallen human natures, but at the same time, they play to and exploit those weaknesses. I never had to be taught to be envious of others and covet their wealth. To learn to be grateful for what I had and not concern myself with how others may have been blessed with material success—that took work. It is work, but it produces real freedom and peace of mind.

Experience has shown me that only about 15 percent of the population has a generous view of life and puts those beliefs into practice. These are the people who volunteer for school, church, and civic committees. They give generously to those in need without seeking thanks or recognition. These are the people that take risks and start businesses. Another 15 percent make up the "renegade" segment of our population. They are looking out for themselves, although the politicians and advocates in this group are the most vocal (and sometimes the most persuasive) that they are not in it for themselves. These takers might look like outlaws or they may be seen in the finest attire. Some may vandalize a neighbor's property, while others might bring down a multinational company with their self-centeredness and recklessness. They may be in prison; they may live in penthouses. The other 70 percent of society is made up of those who are hardworking and somewhat involved. They show up and participate, but they don't really do any heavy lifting (though they often think they do). They can be easily swayed to vote for self-interest over the greater good. It's known as the 15:85 rule: 15 percent of the people in any endeavor will do 85 percent of the giving and contributing. The rest will make smaller contributions or none at all. In our culture activists who have never actually created something or given anything significant from their own resources vilify the 15 percent who are the creators and givers.

In my own times of dependence, I was completely unaware that the warm feeling I got when I received a handout was a snare, a trap. So much that goes along with that dependence is debilitating and entropic. With each abdication of responsibility, an individual loses a little more motivation. When one learns to think this way at a young age or comes from a multigenerational tradition of dependence, it's especially ensnaring. It will almost always require an extraordinary event to find liberation from such dependence—be it an inner conviction, loss of the support, or a conversion experience. Liberation is all the more difficult when those in power have a vested interest in keeping people dependent in order to hold on to that power. Fortunately for me I was released from this entrapment after a few years. This way of thinking would not hold me down for a lifetime; it would not be multigenerational.

When I was growing up, my mother could have simply given up the house, moved us into an apartment, and collected welfare and food stamps. In spite of her own problems, she did not do this. Instead she worked the night shift as a nurse, leaving the house at ten o'clock every night and returning at eight o'clock the next morning. I know my life would have turned out very differently if she had taken what appeared to be an easier way.

In the same way that some lawyers think that for every misfortune in life there should be a lawsuit to compensate for it, the modernist leader thinks that for every misfortune in life, there should be a new government program.

Karl Marx referred to religion as the "opiate of the masses," a statement modernists agree with. However, the satisfaction I received from getting a government check was much more like the warm feeling of a shot of whiskey going down than anything I had ever felt in church up to that point. Handouts to the poor, subsidies to corporations and farmers, outsized union pensions or bailouts, and safety nets for reckless investors are the *real* opiate of the masses!

Some behaviors are uniquely addictive to some and not to others. Some drink socially all their lives without a problem. Some are on the path to alcoholism after a few drinks. One person takes a trip to Las Vegas, throws away a few quarters with the slot machines, and that's it. Someone else quickly starts gambling away his or her paycheck. An opiate is a substance that is almost universally addictive. If opiates are administered to a group of people over time, almost everyone exposed will become addicted. Other substances are not so universally addictive. Opiate addiction, like any other addiction, reduces the addicted to a state of self-centered obsession. The needs of others takes a back seat to the satisfactions and to the needs of the addict.

Monetary dependence can be almost universally addictive, so it can be considered an opiate. Almost all of us have become addicted to the idea of the government providing financial security. The addiction to public largess in our country has become epidemic. As with any addiction it is chronic and progressive. It does not abate with time; it only gets worse.

A country in the heady days of its lapse into modernism is much like the healthy young man or woman that has "discovered" drugs, alcohol, or some other dependency. For a time youthful vitality carries the person along and mitigates, forestalls, or conceals the consequences of the new addiction. Lessons from childhood, remnants of a childhood faith, and a healthy constitution keep the consequences from becoming manifold for some time. Similarly a young country such as the United States that has been grown and nurtured on sound financial principles and functional values can go on for a time without showing the signs of this deleterious and unsustainable system of debt, dependence, and abdication. It's like a sinkhole eroding away the bedrock with little evidence on the surface of the impending collapse until it is too late.

In our country times of hardship have been exploited to ensnare people into dependence. What is a snare? It is simply a baited trap, a trap with some tempting bait. And this bait doesn't appeal to our strengths—it appeals to our weaknesses. This might be old school, but our childhood books warned us of these very weaknesses—stories of wolves in sheep's clothing and enticing gifts that lured people astray. This business of holding out tempting fruit is a pretty old story!

Denying our inherent human weaknesses is part of original sin. (At least we deny the ones that are inconvenient for us to look at.) On the "supply side" of dependence are the power hungry. They are able to fool themselves and others into believing that their motives are pure and that those who oppose them are greedy and evil. Those who are on the receiving end aren't so much in denial; they are into justification. They have a sense of entitlement.

The modernist and humanist influence on our economy is not limited to the welfare state. It's become an urban legend that the power players on Wall Street have an anti-modernist and conservative mind-set. The idea of a Social Darwinist caste system, where some are simply more advanced than others, finds a comfortable home among the financially elite. Recent history has shown, however, that the well-heeled do not mind accepting handouts when they have been reckless and overplayed their hands. Even the early robber barons and industrialists excused living extravagantly with the notion that they were simply humans of a higher order while sending twelve-year-olds into coal mines and sweatshops.

The fruit of choosing courage, truth, and short-term pain is greater strength and vitality and the self-esteem that comes from doing the right things. By choosing the short-term solution of dependence, a loss of independence and pride of accomplishment is displaced by inappropriate dependence and declining self-esteem.

The modernist creed is: "From each according to his ability; to each according to his need."[4] These words sound prosaic and just, but behind these words is a world of ignorance, deceit, and malice. If not for the truths of human nature, these would be inspiring and charitable words. But when applied in a humanist way, apart from the leading of a sovereign God, they have brought about evil of near "cosmic proportions." Apart from that leading, they have opened the floodgates to human destruction.

Why do people borrow recklessly? To live beyond their means? To have pleasures and status that perhaps they weren't intended to have? Why do political leaders borrow? To satisfy their greed for power? To attain and hold on to a degree of control over others that is unnatural? Why do people accept the largess from this unsustainable system that will bring us all to ruin without any pangs of conscience?

---

4 Louis Blanc, 1851; popularized by Karl Marx 1875.

We have become so dependent on the idea of a monolithic government providing for our financial security. We have become easily persuaded by politicians that promise us financial security when they are actually undermining that security. Our oldest and most besetting fear is the fear of financial insecurity, that we will not have enough money to meet our needs. Dependence on a monolithic god like government does seem to take away that fear, but there are consequences for this overdependence. Along with the financial consequences of such an unsustainable system, there is the loss of self-esteem and pride of accomplishment. There is a pall that begins to hang over us as we go from being independent and interdependent to dependency. We lose the sense of vitality of living a life of faith under a just but moderated government. Such a government as this doesn't try to displace God in our lives. We may protest at the thought, but haven't we become a country where all of us to some extent have put aside a vital dependence on our Creator and replaced it with a morbid dependence on modernist leaders? Haven't we chosen modern rulers that are constantly enticing us to put God aside and depend on them, to give our power and identity to them? "We will give up our power, independence and freedom to you if you will take care of us." This is what we have done, this is where we are.

Evidence of the failure of this dependent thinking is that it cannot be sustained and will always result in unsustainable debt. *Unsustainable* is a nice, clean word. It does not give an idea of the massive calamities that follow when a country's economy, so heavily laden with debt, falters and collapses. The modernist leaders that have been responsible for so much economic destruction never seem to have a sense of shame at their failures. They never seem to have a moment of truth. They are never contrite, for real contrition does not come when you are a "god."

The Decline and Fall of the American Empire: Most Americans think if there were a book by this title it could only be metaphorical, a book describing some aspect of our lives that the author thinks has passed. We do not think there could be a total economic collapse of America as a country. We do not think that what happened to the Roman Empire could happen to us. The Romans never imagined that their economy and culture would totally collapse either.

Reality shows about "preppers" have become popular—shows about individuals and families that are preparing for some form of social and economic upheaval. We watch these shows and think they are interesting and the preppers themselves quirky, but we think it could never happen here, not really. Yet even though we think that the scenarios the preppers imagine will not actually come about, we have a gnawing sense that they may be right. We have become blind to the lessons of history. We are in a state of denial. We are unable to clearly see that debt, radical self-interest, and moral anarchy have undermined all of our social and financial foundations to the point that it is only a matter of time before some event not of our own choosing will reveal these mortal weakness. When we reach that point, it will be too late to correct the problem. It will then be too late to listen to unheeded warnings. The Rhine will have frozen over, and all will be lost.

We appear to be enthralled and mesmerized by the ever-growing and all-intrusive presence of our government, its tentacles reaching into every aspect of life. We don't see that the monstrous debt that it has created will turn on us and devour us.

In the last months of my addiction to alcohol and drugs, I had just graduated college and was looking for my first job, that foot in the door in my chosen profession. Hundreds of resumes and many interviews resulted in the offer of a minimum wage job with no benefits at a local architectural firm. It was during the time I worked there, however, that my experience of Grace came about. A few months later I found myself laid off and unemployed, but now I possessed a new attitude about work, money, and dependence. Out of force of habit, I filed for unemployment benefits. After taking a week off, I drove to the town of Red Bank where several architectural firms were located. I parked my car and set out to go door to door with a little prayer. "OK, Lord, let's see what you have for me today." I was hired at the first office I visited.

I kept my appointment at the unemployment office the next week. When the interviewer looked at my paperwork and saw only one job inquiry, she asked "What is this?" I responded that I got a job and was only there to receive a check for the two weeks I was out of work. An experience of Grace and a few months of spiritual growth had produced a dramatic change in my attitudes and actions about money. I changed from someone who thought the world owed him a living to someone that could take pride in supporting myself and giving to others.

This experience of Grace affected my attitudes on all levels. I was no longer someone that borrowed without really planning to pay it back. I went from being a taker to someone that had surplus and could give to others in need, from someone with a sense of entitlement and misplaced dependencies to someone with a sense of security about my finances that didn't come from the government.

Our nation needs a similar sense of security and momentum in our economy that doesn't come from the government.

We need not be without hope. God has given us a world of problems and solutions, vice and virtue, waste and prudence, deceit and honesty, pride and humility, denial and truth. We simply need to abandon the former and adopt the latter. If we do this, God will then provide the needed guidance and power. I have found this to be true in my own life.

Proceeding forward with honesty, courage, wisdom, thrift, and prudence will restore our nation's empty coffers. More importantly it will restore peace and something of real brotherhood and sisterhood to our land.

What works to restore the life of an individual will work to restore a family, a village, a community, a culture. The only difference is scale.

"We should not forget that it will be just as important to our descendants to be prosperous in their time as it is to us to be prosperous in our time."
THEODORE ROOSEVELT

"Submit to God and be at peace with him;
in this way prosperity will come to you."
THE POCKET COMPANION BIBLE NKJV

EIGHT

MODERN LOVE

"The great danger for family life, in the midst of any society whose idols are pleasure, comfort and independence, lies in the fact that people close their hearts and become selfish. . . . The worst prison is a closed heart."
ST. JOHN PAUL II

"Recognize the truth that there is in ourselves something incomparably more precious than what we perceive externally."
ST. TERESA OF AVILA

WHAT BECOMES OF romantic love in the world of modernism? How does modernism affect our families and closest relationships? What happens when everyone decides for himself or herself what is right and what is wrong? When we no longer see each other as created in the image and likeness of our Creator, precious in His sight and dearly loved by Him, but instead as soulless, evolved creatures? When radical self-interest governs our behavior?

Paterson, New Jersey, is an nineteenth-century textile milling town. Like other New Jersey manufacturing towns, tidy row houses line the narrow streets. The textile industry is long gone now, and the mills have been converted to condominiums for New York City commuters. The rest of the city consists of impoverished, low-income housing.

Our Lady of Victories Church is an inner-city parish in the low-income area. It has been added onto over the years, with the most recent addition being the early twentieth-century sanctuary. The oldest section over 150 years old. The restoration of these buildings was my first large commission when I started my own architectural practice.

With my previous employer I had been involved in the restoration of the Cathedral of St. John the Baptist for the Diocese of Paterson. My working relationships from that commission led to this project. The restoration work required the use of brownstone, which is actually a sandstone. Some sections of Our Lady of Victories Church were so badly deteriorated and eroded that they resembled melted wax creations. My team and I started this project with building forensics. We went over the buildings from top to bottom, outside to inside, to determine the scope and nature of the remedial work.

Like many inner-city churches, there was a daycare center in the facility. As I walked around to survey building conditions, passing the fenced yard for the daycare center, I noticed a group of young boys. Some of them called out to me, "Daddy, Daddy." I was startled that these boys would call me, a stranger, Daddy. It was heartbreakingly obvious that these young boys were without the love of a father and were desperate for that love. This is another unfortunate result of modernism. According to the sexual mores of the modernists, the family is an outdated institution and we should all express our sexuality freely. This has damaged these young boys and the millions like them in our country and around the world.

I worked on this project over twenty-five years ago. Those young boys would be grown men now. I am afraid that for want of the love of a father and an intact family, the lives they are living today do not contain as much joy, fulfillment, or freedom as they might have.

Modernism's "new" sexual freedom may have provided some pleasure without guilt to the stronger and the affluent. The modernist leaders have enjoyed the sense of self-aggrandizement and self-satisfaction of their supposed moral superiority. This freedom may appear to be without consequences, but it has been as crushing as it has been seductive for those that have been less prepared to deal with it.

"If It Feels Good, Do It"

Chad (not his real name) was a grade school friend of my son. When we met, he was in fifth grade and had already buried three parents.

One had died of a drug overdose and the other of suicide shortly after that. He was brought to New Jersey and adopted by his aunt and her husband. A few short years later his aunt, his adoptive mother, succumbed to breast cancer.

Chad and my son don't see much of each other since leaving the small Christian grade school they attended together. They have graduated from high school now. Whenever I see Chad around town, I encourage him to stop in for a visit. He took me up on my invitation one afternoon and stopped by with his current girlfriend. They were looking for a place to stay. His girlfriend was afraid to go home to her abusive father for fear of being beaten. She shared with me that she wasn't sure her father—the man married to her mother—was actually her biological father. Her mother had been sleeping with his brother as well when she became pregnant with their daughter.

Free love and free sex have not served these young people very well.

Some time ago I traveled back to New Orleans to visit Malcolm, an old college friend. He was someone I spent a lot of time drinking and drugging with during my time there. I was fortunate to have made it out of that town alive. In the early eighties, New Orleans was rife with drugs and violence. I spent one summer working construction on a "shotgun" house owned by a drug dealer. When the workers started taking off their shirts in the stifling New Orleans summer heat, most of them had multiple gunshot scars.

Malcolm and I had stayed in touch over the years even though our lives had gone in divergent directions. I had put off this visit for a few years, wanting to be more comfortable in my new life before being around all of that again. Like most other shotgun houses in New Orleans, Malcolm's was just a string of rooms front to back with no hallway. Similar to a train with multiple cars, one had to pass through one room to get to the next.

I knocked on the side door, and a voice called, "It's open." Inside I was greeted by Malcolm and his companion in bed together. Since college Malcolm had joined the gay community; he was still heavily involved in buying and selling drugs, and now he had AIDS.

Our conversation that day was mostly about gay life in New Orleans in the eighties. A constant flow of customers came and went, purchasing cocaine and Quaaludes. Another college friend, now a physician, was kept busy dispensing regulated AIDS medications. Malcolm's weekly bridge club was down to one survivor: Malcolm. His brother, a male escort to corporate executives, had died in his arms a few years earlier of the same disease. Violence against and amongst gays was rampant. He told me the most violent and bloody homicides were gay on gay.

Malcolm asked about my life and invited me to share about my faith. This began a dialog that continued over the following months until his disease progressed and we lost touch with each other. His life was very unstable—he moved from boyfriend to boyfriend every few months. The last contact I had with him was a message he left with my wife: "Tell Michael I'm heading out to church." I think he might have appreciated having a friend outside the gay lifestyle that cared for him just for who he was and not because it was fashionable to say you had gay friends with AIDS in the 1980s.

It is not for any of us to judge, but it appears that modernism has taken what was intended to bring the most pleasure and intimacy to our lives and turned it into the source of much suffering, heartache, sickness, and death.

Often the modernists act as though they invented sex. It's as though all that went before was oppressive and destructive and stifling. If we are honest, we have to acknowledge that, however flawed and imperfect in practice, the traditional wisdom provided more security and safety. Any truly scientific, empirical review of the sexual revolution reveals that it has brought about a worldwide epidemic of sickness, disease, and heartache.

The Fallacy of Pro-Choice

"I have done something that I can't undo. There was someone that wanted to help, but I didn't call them. I just went ahead and did it, and now it can't be undone."

It has been twenty years since I sat next to a woman and listened as she spoke these words with great anguish. It still chills me to think of her pain that day. Most of the abortion stories I've heard have been similar. Often the boyfriend lovingly counsels his girlfriend, "It's the right thing to do at this time. I'll support you—I'll go with you." Too often that boyfriend doesn't show up to meet her for the appointment or disappears shortly afterward.

At the peaceful pro-life demonstrations at abortion clinics, I've seen men that do show up, full of righteous indignation, pushing their way through the crowd to get their girlfriend into the clinic—as if *modern chivalry* was escorting one's girlfriend or wife to her abortion. Are these "pro-choice" men really being selfless and caring, or are they just taking a position that will get them what they want and then spare them any consequences and responsibility later on? How is it possible that the "*Playboy* philosophy" and radical feminism agree on this subject?

On a deeper level, how does one philosophically, morally, and logically embrace the pro-choice position? For it to be a "choice," we have to completely take away the humanity of the child in the womb. If there is humanity there, this can't be a simple choice; there must be some protection. Believing that a growing fetus (Latin for "small person") has no humanity requires the worldview that a child is something other than a person, completely without rights. One has to be completely divorced from truth, science, reason, and morality to believe this modernist view of mankind in the womb.

We have wonderful technology available to us now that gives us the ability to see the developing child in the womb in all his or her beauty and innocence. The modernist looks at that child and says, "No, you are nothing. You are no more than trash that can be disposed of at my command. Not only will I let you be destroyed, I will destroy those that will try to save you." There is no colder, cruel, or more arrogant position than this.

Some women identify having an abortion as an event that led to trouble with drugs, alcohol, and relationships. The pro-abortion activists deny the existence of the Post Abortion Syndrome, a post-traumatic stress disorder. Unable to face reality, they fill the airwaves, broadband, and print media with a constant inundation of denial and propaganda. In doing so, they deter women (and men) from finding acceptance and healing for what they have been through. By denying the truth, they block women (and men) from facing reality and being able to forgive themselves and those that pressured them into an abortion.

One previous president of the United States has always been militantly pro-abortion. As an Illinois legislator he was the only politician, Democrat or Republican, to take the floor to oppose legislation that would make it illegal to kill a child that has survived a late-term abortion. Politicians take such positions and then call anyone with pro-life inclinations "extremist." What leaders say, do, and believe matters. When morally ambiguous messages such as this are sent out to the young and impressionable, especially those who are at risk, we shouldn't be surprised when we have instances of children killing children.

In the public debates, young people can't help but see diagrams of how babies are killed with a scissor stab to the back of the neck in partial-birth abortions. They also can't escape seeing our most powerful leaders defending such practices. These are not images that should be part of anyone's childhood experience. These are discussions we should not even be having.

About the time our first child was born, while my wife and son were still in the hospital, there was a story in the news about an abortionist that had been gunned down. The abortionist, ironically named Gunn, specialized in late-term abortions. As I was sitting in the neonatal unit, I thought about the moral ambiguity of the modernist argument for abortion. If someone came into that unit with the intent to kill the premature babies being cared for there, anyone who took him out would be a hero. Dr. Gunn was killing healthy and viable babies, in abortions of convenience, at the same level of development. How is someone considered a hero for using deadly force to stop a killing in one instance, yet a villain in another? This is not to condone violence but to illustrate the terribly confused morality of the modernist.

When abortion was legalized and accepted, we ignored the warnings of moral philosophers that this form of violence would beget increased violence in other forms. Devaluing human life in one form devalues it in all other forms. We can now clearly see that these moral philosophers were right in their predictions.

The sexual revolution is not a movement that came about spontaneously. It started with relatively few activists who put forth very simple ideas that changed how we view each other and the beautifully complex and incredibly fragile human embryo and how it comes to be. Activists promoted the idea that there is no Creator of the universe who has laid out precepts for us to live by. The simple idea that we don't have a corrupt nature that will lead us to our ruin if we are left to our own devices. They claimed their new ideals would set us

MODERN LOVE | 75

free and deliver women from abuse and repression. These ideals may provide enjoyments for a few, without apparent consequences, but the net return has been more abuse of men, women, and children. The modernist view of mankind turns men in to users and consumers and women into products.

It is at our own peril that we ignore God's loving guidance and follow our own selfish nature. Left to our own devices apart from God's grace, our evening news will always be filled with calamities. I think many would return to their senses if not for modernism's constant propaganda and prevarications.

The basic modernist view is that ever greater sexual freedom is progressive and fulfilling. Acceptance of almost all sexual practices is likewise progressive, accepting, and compassionate. It is the moral high ground. The negative consequences of all this sexual activity is either denied or the solution is yet more progressive thinking. Any mention of restraint is considered backwards, judgmental, and self-righteous. Modernists have been thoroughly effective in their propaganda. Anyone who speaks of modesty or prudence in any public setting is instantly castigated. Though these are ways of thinking we need to revisit.

What modernists believe to be *progress* is in truth *decline*.

For most of Western history, we have been admonished to not envy, covet, or lust after others or their possessions. These tendencies represent the weaker side of our humanity, and as such they are the areas where we are easily seduced. We can be easily convinced that what is bad for us is good.

Modern love, modern romance, modern relationships . . . as with most of modernism, propaganda comes at us through media outlets, slanted news programs and documentaries, and emotional arguments. Modernists believe that the sexual revolution is just natural progression, but it's not really natural at all. And now the most seductive, addictive, and harmful behaviors have been given the legitimacy of science. But what if it is not really science at all? Maybe all these elites have just been blinded by these age-old deceptions and have brought millions along with them. Somewhere along the way vice and virtue became inverted. Somehow vice became virtue and the purveyors of vice the heroes and the champions of virtue the villains.

Modernism's ideas on the material has wrecked economies. Their ideas on sex and relationships have destroyed untold hearts, minds, and bodies. We desperately need higher ideals. We must pursue the timeless ideals that protect the weak and innocent. The alternative is to continue to cause great harm to ourselves and others.

Modernists have convinced us that the classical virtues are oppressive. They are not. Some of the classical virtues are temperance, prudence, courage, and justice. In regards to sexuality we could add modesty, restraint, gentleness, and tenderness of heart. The list could go on. This is not oppression. It is how we show real love and respect for each other and all those affected by our behavior. It is how we show gratitude for this very wonderful and special gift we have been given by our Creator.

We do not need to be without hope. We don't need to treat ourselves and others in such hurtful and destructive ways. The answers have been given to us; they are right in front of us. Most of us know in our quiet moments what those answers are. We must simply acknowledge at the deepest societal levels that we are way off track. If we do, God will provide the strength and direction we need.

> *"Love is patient, love is kind. It does not envy, it does not boast,*
> *it is not proud. It does not dishonor others, it is not self-seeking,*
> *it is not easily angered, it keeps no record of wrongs. Love does not*
> *delight in evil but rejoices with the truth. It always protects,*
> *always trusts, always hopes, always perseveres."*
> 1 CORINTHIANS 13:4-7, NEW INTERNATIONAL VERSION *(NIV)*

NINE

BUCHAREST

"Stealing from capitalism is not like stealing out of our own pockets. Marx and Lenin have taught us that anything is ethical, so long as it is in the interest of the proletarian class and it's world revolution"
"The fetus is the property of the whole society. Anyone having children is a deserter who abandons the laws of national continuity."
MODERNIST DICTATOR NICOLAE CEAUSESCU

" The people, they are like worms; no matter how much you feed them, they are always hungry."
ELENA CEAUSESCU, WIFE OF MODERNIST DICTATOR NICOLAE CEAUSESCU

WE LANDED IN the middle of the night in Bucharest, where we were greeted by a driver from the adoption agency who would take us to our hotel. After throwing our bags in the trunk, we raced off into the night in true Eastern European fashion. I had been in Romania less than an hour, but I was pretty certain that the sign we just flew past as we drove onto the ramp meant "One Way—Do Not Enter."

We were in Bucharest to finalize the adoption process and bring home our middle daughter. The usual process was to fly in the day before the paper work and examinations were to begin and then rush through the next five days of agencies and orphanages. We had decided to add time at the beginning and end of the process in order to get to know our new daughter in her homeland before heading home to ours.

At the front end of the trip, we got over our jet lag while enjoying the hospitality of a pastor in Prague, Czech Republic. His church was affiliated with local churches in New Jersey, so we had met before. The pastor's father was also a preacher and had spent most of his life in Communist prisons for the crime of telling people about the Good Shepherd. They had finished a new parsonage on donated land and the concrete shell for their new church was up. As a successful church architect, I try to give back to church projects in countries that don't enjoy the prosperity that we do. I have supported several projects in former Eastern Bloc countries. I am always amazed that these projects in former Communist countries, with a heavy remnant of their former ways, have much less bureaucracy to deal with than we do when trying to build things here in America. I worked with a pastor here in New Jersey that had left Communist Romania. The first pastorate he had here was with a church that was beginning a building project. His comment on the planning board approval process was, "I thought I left this all behind in communist Romania."

The pastor we were visiting had been present during the nonviolent "Velvet Revolution" that overthrew Communism in his country. He became a respected civic leader and had been elected mayor of his quarter of Prague.

Ten years is not a very long time to recover from eighty years of oppression, propaganda, and indoctrination, overrun in turn by both Communists and Nazis, two ideologies that are usually characterized as opposing but really share the same progressive humanist pedigree. There was a coldness and seriousness about the people in Prague and a spiritual chill in the air. The pastor told us that it takes years of meeting with an individual to win his or her trust after decades of anti-Christian propaganda. Propaganda very similar to that which fills our airwaves and printed media.

Our guide and driver while we were in Romania was a young Romanian. He was old enough to remember Communism and was now a political science student is the US. He told us, "We used to wait in line for bread, now we wait in line for cell phones." A medieval fort on a near mountaintop was now conquered by cell phone towers.

We also visited the Museum of Rural Life in Bucharest. The recreated village is similar to Colonial Williamsburg. The outside section is a parklike setting with cottages from the different regions of Romania. The pre-Communist cottages are all very unique according to the local culture and climate. They are unlike the universal sameness of typical Communist construction. Some were underground structures for insulation, and others were built on piles with the barn below. Some were embellished on every surface of the exterior with carvings of vines and flowers. None were more than a few hundred square feet. At the crossroads of the connecting trails were the religious shrines that would have been found at the intersection of rural cart paths. The indoor museum displayed traditional rural life. Each region had its own costume—each one as splendid and colorful and vibrant as ever, even after decades of the grayness of Communism. We found the display in the basement to be the most interesting. Here we saw artifacts from Romania's Communist past, everyday items people would have had in their homes. What struck me the most was how tacky Soviet Communism could be. Communist kitsch; Communist tchotchke. Porcelain, gilded lamp bases, and ashtrays with busts of Lenin and Stalin.

Aside from the artifacts of the Communist era, we saw current, political works of art. A Styrofoam head that one would usually see in a department store to display a hat or wig was wearing a Communist party beret. The beret and Styrofoam head were displayed within a steel cage—a statement to party members not being the free thinkers they fancied themselves to be.

This glimpse into Communism revealed the fallacy of yet another hallmark of modernism: the belief that its adherents are progressive free-thinkers and seekers of truth. But take away the emotion and jargon, and there is only dull stasis. There is always an air of self-righteousness and intellectual vanity about modernist movements, whether here or abroad. Even though there is always ample evidence that modernism is tremendously destructive, its proponents move on with their noses up in the air.

Our hotel was in the embassy district of Bucharest. Bucharest had at one time, before Communism, been considered the Paris of Eastern Europe. The older architecture here is unique and elegant—or it used to be. As with the decayed housing in our inner cities, one has to look past the rough repairs, layers of off-color paint, and aluminum-sided soffits to see the charm and delight that once was there. Most of the nicer homes from the pre-modernist era were either given over for use by Communist officials or repurposed for use by the state. We saw one large wood frame home, similar to our shingle style but with the elegance of the Queen

Anne style (though still eastern European in feel). It had lost its glow and was painted over from top to bottom with an off-the-shelf dark brown gloss. Like the many older homes of our cities, the details were covered up. As with the decayed housing in our inner cities, it is not the loss of architectural gems that saddens me so much as the loss of a way of life that itself had charm, delight, and freedom—a way of life that has been replaced by an emptiness and ever-present, domineering malevolence.

There was a concrete wall of newer construction around this particular property. Peering over to the courtyard, we observed the saddest sight of all. This home had been put to use as an orphanage for older abandoned teens, ones that have no hope of adoption.

When Communism fell in Romania and our media entered the country, they made much of Ceausescu's efforts to pressure all Romanians to have more children even though they couldn't be taken care of. They tried to make some sort of perverse connection between this and the pro-life movement in America, as if the pro-life movement would force people to have children and lots of them. In truth, this is just what modernists do: control, coerce, and micromanage. In one country, they pressure families to have more children, and, in another, they restrict or pressure them not to.

The plaza outside Ceausescu's palace was huge and empty. The vast plaza was designed for mass gatherings of his dependents who were "invited" to come and hear their leader proselytize from his balcony 150 feet above. Totalitarian architecture is always designed to be impersonal and imposing. Somehow "The People's Palace" ended up being just one man's colossal residence.

The boulevard extending on a straight axis from this Communist palace proved to be another example of modernist kitsch. The middle of the lane was filled with fountains and stucco dolphins. The main boulevard had been under construction when Communism was overthrown, and the construction stopped abruptly. As we moved from the completed sections near the palace and drove away we saw where construction ended. Aside from the rust on the scaffolding and the exposed steel rebar, it appeared as if the workmen were just away on a lunch break, although it had been over ten years. The workers literally stopped working and walked away.

In constructing this monument to himself, Ceausescu ordered the residential neighborhoods to be leveled in order to construct the formal boulevard. Prior to the French Revolution, the bourgeoisie did the same in constructing their grand palaces. Entire neighborhoods of peasant housing would be leveled to create the perfect axis of formal lanes and gardens. Two hundred years later the movement of "fraternity, equality, and brotherhood" has come back to be what they thought they were destroying with the lopping off of a few hundred heads. All the blood and carnage couldn't change human nature. Communists couldn't root out from their own hearts the very things that they were revolting against. The obsession with power corrupts thoroughly, whether it expresses itself in the gilded Versailles or brutish statists overarching and infiltrating every aspect of human life.

Modernists deny the unpleasant and immutable realities of human nature, at least in themselves. In their arrogance they cannot see the corruption in their own hearts. They believe they can engineer and manage human nature. In the end the denial leads to the enflaming of all things they believe they oppose. The same greed and oppression they say they see in orthodox religion and free market societies shows up tenfold in their own movements.

We passed through their mountain skiing resort area. A lighted iron cross that had been removed by the Communists had been restored to its place on the top of the rock outcropping overlooking the town. Litigating to remove religious images from public places has become a popular pastime for modernist legal activists in our country.

A roadside memorial commemorated the British airmen that had been shot down during bombing runs over this area. It had been one of the Nazis' primary sources of petroleum and an important and extremely dangerous target for the allies. I don't think I saw a memorial marker for any officer or enlisted man that was more than twenty-three years old when he sacrificed his life.

During our time in Romania, we were traveling with another couple; they were from Ohio and there to adopt a boy, John Paul, who would turn six on the day they picked him up at an orphanage supported by the Ronald McDonald House. We were with them as they went through a brief process of signing him out. In the play yard we were surrounded by young boys around the same age as John Paul. I got down on my knee to tie my shoe and instantly become a human jungle gym. All the boys all want to be touched and held, to be taken home and have a father and mother.

Our daughter Bethany is an orphaned gypsy from the Hungarian-speaking area of Romania. There is a prejudice against gypsies here that we were not familiar with. They are shunned and despised by others in all walks of life. Doctors, lawyers, or pastors—they were all appalled that we are actually adopting a gypsy. It's true that the gypsies do tend to be involved in much illicit activity, and this has contributed to the stigma.

As we got closer to the village where our daughter was staying with her foster family, we passed an odd site: a reservoir with a church steeple rising up from its middle. Our guide told us that in order to build the reservoir, the Communists simply dammed up and flooded the valley, leaving the church steeple and a few other roofs sticking up from the water line.

Bethany (Bazsa, her given Romanian name) was living with her foster parents on their family's ancestral farm. With the advent of Communism, all farms were taken from individuals and given to the collectives. We had passed some of the abandoned barracks of the collectives on our way north, with combines rusting in the fields. Bazsa's foster parents had their house and a small plot in the village. Return of the upper pastures to their rightful owners was still tied up. Bazsa's foster parents looked as though they have lived a life of struggles. They looked at least ten years older than me, and I was surprised to find they actually were younger than me.

We didn't have much time with them, but we enjoyed their hospitality for a while. They shared what little they had; local treats and cakes were prepared for us. Bethany's foster grandmother made hats and wall hangings for us from woven straw, and we still count these among our prized possessions.

The little mustachioed ladies of the village with their kerchief-covered heads came out to wave good-bye as we drove away with Bethany. Everyone we encountered was either delighted for or envious of someone who could leave and go to America.

We headed south back to Bucharest. At a McDonald's in Transylvania, Bethany got her first Happy Meal. She was terrified and traumatized by us—strange people that didn't speak her language and were driving her away from what had been family and home for a few months. She had just turned three, but she had experienced more difficulty and abandonment in those few years than many who were much older. Arriving at the hotel I tried to put her shoes on with her kicking and screaming. My watch broke and snapped off my wrist. *This isn't going to be easy*, I thought.

Back Home

After a few months back home, we took our now family of six to Spruce Lake Retreat, a Mennonite campground and retreat center. The Mennonites and the Amish come from the same traditions and background, but while Mennonites also have a separatist way of life, they do not eschew technology. Spruce Lake Retreat is a very safe and quite place, with hiking trails going past the waterfall and up to the top of Spruce Mountain. It's one of the few places where we don't worry if we haven't seen our young children for an hour or so, much like the neighborhood in New Jersey where I grew up. Now we have to escape to a Mennonite retreat in the mountains of Pennsylvania to enjoy the same community many of us used to enjoy in our own neighborhoods.

Modernists talk much about community and "building community," but this is not something that can be synthesized by bureaucrats, "community organizers," or activists. It can only be created by people nurturing it themselves over generations and defending it from those with evil intent. It cannot be had by those that have abdicated control and responsibility for their futures and the maintenance of the fabric of their community to centralized government. It can't be found where individuals are unwilling to face the nature of their problems honestly, pity themselves, blame others, waste time and energy envying others, and refuse to take responsibility for themselves.

This type of community is the farthest thing from modernism, yet at the same time it is what modernism seeks to create in its own way. Modernists try to create utopias here on earth with their top-down management and forced equality. But what is required of all individuals in a beautiful community is an abundance of character and selfless devotion to each other. Modernism by its very nature is barren in this respect and, all propaganda to the contrary only promotes, fosters, and even rewards the most selfish and self-centered behavior.

We were here at Spruce Lake Retreat for "Family Week." It hadn't been going well with our adopted daughter in the months since we brought her home, and most every day has been a struggle against defiance.

At the retreat we became friends with another family. The wife was from Romania and told us her story. She met her engineer husband when he was on assignment in Communist Romania. Petitioning the government to be allowed to leave, she was allowed to go, provided she left within twenty-four hours, only taking what fit in a small suitcase. As a young child she had been taken from her family to be raised by the state. There was something about her countenance that told us she had been shaken and broken at her core. We talk much about different forms of abuse but little about abuse of the young by the state. Like most abusers the state can have a delusional belief that they are in some form helping the ones they are actually harming.

In our country, to a large degree, we have abdicated the raising of our children to the state, public education, and popular culture. To just the extent that we have done this have our communities become unmanageable.

During our short stay in a former Soviet Bloc country, we saw a Christian pastor elected to public office, an anti-Communist art display, crosses restored to places of public prominence, and a church built in a residential neighborhood with little or no bureaucratic resistance. Why did we have to go to Eastern Europe to get a refreshing dose of political, religious, and artistic freedom? Here at home the heavy, leaden blanket of political correctness would be dropped over all of this.

There is a "spirit of modernism," and it spreads across the world like a plague of ideas. It has been a plague that brings more indiscriminate pain and misery than any physical plague that has visited the human race.

How can we give our children a future of real peace and security? By abandoning the ways of modernism and humbly following the simpler ways of wisdom, faith, hope, and charity.

"Of course, I grew up in Communist Romania, but I am happy to say that now our country is democratic and prospering, since the revolution of 1989."
NADIA COMENICI

"For us in Russia, communism is a dead dog, while, for many people in the West, it is still a living lion."
ALEKSANDR SOLZHENITSYN

TEN

ARE WE THERE YET?

"You will never reach your destination if you stop and throw rocks at every dog that barks."
WINSTON CHURCHILL

WHEN PEOPLE ARE miserable and discontented, characteristically they are unable to be happy with their current circumstances and their current means. They always believe that some imagined future event, something outside themselves, will make them happy. When they move to a new state, buy a new house, or acquire a new spouse, *then* they will be happy. On the other hand, happy people, although they may have goals and dreams for the future, know that in order to be happy today, they need to accept their circumstances and live in the now. People who are addicted to alcohol are unhappy in their circumstances but have an ongoing delusion that they will be happy and able to drink normally when some imagined future circumstance comes about. However, even if these circumstances do come about, such individuals will not be happy. They won't be happy because they can't accept the truth about themselves, and they blame others for their circumstances.

Being unable to be content and happy with life goes hand in hand with self-pity. A person can't be happy, productive, or free by having such attitudes, and neither can a society. Those who have abdicated personal responsibility are especially vulnerable to charismatic leaders, whether it's a cult leader, religious leader, or politician. It's easy to get hold of people's hearts and minds by reinforcing their self-pity and blaming others for their troubles. It is easy to persuade them that they are justified in feeling this way. It is just as easy to persuade them that they will be happy when the next election is won and the new program implemented. Such a person caters to and takes advantage of people by reinforcing their self-pity and other negative attitudes in order to advance their political career. What becomes of a nation that uses this as a basis for governance? What happens after decades of reinforcing these attitudes and continually promising more and more benefits to satisfy people that can't be satisfied? The result is generations of promises and benefits that can't possibly be sustained. While not limited to modernist leaders, it is always the centerpiece of their campaigns.

These same attitudes and beliefs that will bring down an individual will bring down a family, a community, or a culture. The higher beliefs and attitudes that serve to elevate a person also will elevate a people and an empire. Good attitudes and beliefs are good attitudes whether they are on a micro or mega scale.

Always Wanting More

Some people can't be content with their current financial circumstances. They think they need more things to be content or feel important. They borrow and rack up debt they can never pay off in order to maintain prestige. They have a delusion that someday some imagined windfall will come through and they will be able to get out from under it all.

The modernist leader, in order to maintain power and prestige, always promises more benefits, which only adds up to more ruinous debt. They likewise seem to suffer from the delusion that some imagined future circumstance will somehow make the debt go away.

Consider a father who likes to see himself in a certain way. He takes great pride in providing the best for his family. This is all well and good as long as he actually has the means to pay for these things without incurring unreasonable debt or conducting his affairs in an unethical way to achieve those ends. But what if he doesn't actually have the earning capacity to provide as he would like to? What happens if he once did but for whatever reason his income has diminished? He has promised his kids the best vacations, schools, cars and clothing. If he can't humbly accept his circumstances and be honest with his family, he will incur debt to maintain the image of himself that he desires. Maybe he will start to behave unethically to try and catch up.

At any time he has the option to stop and admit that he has over-promised and simply can't deliver what he thought he could. If he has taught his children that they can be happy at any income level, this may be received by his family graciously. If he has taught his kids to be envious of others, blame others for misfortune, or feel entitled, his children might turn their backs on him in disgust. It's hard to think of parents actually teaching their children self-pity and blame shifting as a way of life, but it is common these days. It's hard to think of the leaders of our country actually promoting self-pity, envy, and discontent, but that's been the case for quite some time. In their desire for power and prestige, they have promised more than they can deliver, and the truly weak and needy are trampled underfoot by others scrambling for more and more benefits and payouts.

Modernism and its adherents are not so much unlike the discontent-ed and maladjusted that can't find happiness and wholeness in their current circumstances. They can't adopt a few timeless proverbial prin-ciples, live accordingly, and accept life on life's terms. They can't accept that they are not the rulers of the universe and there are things that are simply out of their control and beyond their understanding. Each new campaign is about how bad and unjust things are and how much hap-pier everyone will be when such and such program is advanced. There is an ongoing delusion that all this will lead to some man-made utopia.

Too often our country is being run on the basis of who can ferment the most bitterness and discontent and then in turn promise the most benefits to satisfy the discontented. You need only look at supporters of modernism to see how this plays out—they are a pretty bitter and sour bunch.

Modernist dialog is not so much unlike the cacophony that goes on in the mind of the addict or alcoholic. However, there is something that goes on in the mind of the alcoholic that you'll never hear from the lips of a modernist leader: There is never an expression of guilt or remorse for the tremendous failures and suffering they have caused. Being a modernist means never having to say you are sorry.

With every election cycle, we are presented with a new crisis. If the modernists don't have the good fortune, for them, to have a real crisis such as an economic downturn or a natural or man-made catastrophe, they invent one or magnify an existing one greatly. The program that expands their power is the only solution to the impending calamity, according to them. It is always a program that expands, never diminishes, their power. It is rare that there is a real grassroots movement or a natural groundswell of support for the cause of the day. Eventually there may be a large base of support for their cause but only after a large investment in massive propaganda campaigns. Sometimes it will require decades of a constant maelstrom of emotional arguments before the elite few can gain the bare minimum of support to advance their cause by legislation or judicial fiat.

We hear there will be dire consequences if the modernist's policy is not advanced and made into law. We are told in no uncertain terms that those who oppose their legislation are the most lowly of creatures—selfish and only trying to take care of those who already have too much.

Modernists never tell us what the end game is. They seem to be in pursuit of some sort of utopia, but we are not given the specifics of what this utopia looks like. When will there be enough government programs to solve all of the problems they perceive? How much tax should individuals and entities ideally pay? They won't tell us. Shouldn't there be some sort of *blueprint*? How much government is too much government? Can the modernists ever honestly answer that question?

There are answers to these questions. For many of us the answer is that we already have way too much government. But in a more empirical sense, there is a tipping point when there is more government than can be sustained. There is a point when a majority of the electorate is dependent on government. With dependents having a majority, the only leaders that will be electable will be those that will increase benefits to the dependent majority. When we reach this point, there are no longer any checks and balances. Our "treasury" is then completely empty and burdened with debt. Then it is only a matter of time before circumstances beyond our control reveal the weakness of our condition and our culture and our nation cease to exist as we know it. We may very well be beyond the point of no return already.

We have been going down this road for some eighty-plus years in our country, and we don't seem to be any closer to a solution. Our problems are only compounding. At this point in our history, all the indicators of what make for a healthy society are on the decline. There is more violence and abuse. There is more government debt—debt that is not sustainable or survivable. There is less brotherly love and more fear than trust.

In the frenzy and constant bombardment of propaganda, real problems that present a clear and present danger are overlooked. Those who point out that modernist ideas have brought about these problems are demonized. This is not unlike a group of petulant juveniles that have formed their own code of conduct which will end in the destruction of others and themselves.

The motives of moral vanity, self-righteous aggrandizement, sanctimony, and a craven lust for power and control drives modernism on. There is real and sometimes almost unstoppable power in these age-old seductions. Simply put, the end result is *denial, debt, dependence,* and *decadence.*

Each generation has its own struggles, its own weaknesses and strengths. The empires of the past that we look to for inspiration had their times of advancement, both culturally and economically. None of these empires are in existence today. For the most part they were all conquered from within, not from without. If they were conquered from without, it was after becoming weak from within.

If we lived in harmony with the design and plan of our Creator, there would be much less suffering in this life. It will never be eliminated—there will always be suffering and calamity in this world. There will always be hardship. To accept these hardships without abdicating our responsibilities or blaming others is the challenge we face.

Because modernists are unable to accept the truths about human nature, they are unable to accept "life on life's terms." As a lawyer sees an opportunity to sue whenever the inevitable misfortunes of life occur, so the modernist sees an opportunity to exploit any crisis to expand their power and their agenda.

We all would like to solve the ills of poverty and war. And there are things that can be done. These involve courage, generosity, wisdom, and prudence. They involve selflessness, not selfishness. We need a broader and deeper view of these situations in order to be truly helpful and not cause a deleterious effect on the supposed recipients of relief.

The test of whether an action is good or bad is simple. Does the action or legislation impart more power to the supposed benefactor, and is the sacrifice really on their part?

It's time for those who have supported these programs over the decades to ask, "Are we there yet? Why aren't we there yet?" There have been eighty-plus years of modernist overhaul of our culture, but there seems to be more discontent than ever.

With modernism, however, there is no "there" to reach for two reasons. The first is that we live in a flawed and fallen world where there will never be a man-made utopia. We can only strive to have governance that will follow timeless precepts and proverbial wisdom to get us to the place of the greatest peace and prosperity as is humanly possible. The second is that with flawed, man-centered modernist ideology, the only "there" is a place that is corrupt, dishonest, and delusional and only contains more discontent, more fractured communities, and ruinous debt.

For an equal amount of time that modernism has been remaking our basic form of government, it has also been changing how we think about and relate to each other—not only in our personal and intimate relations, but in our basic civic relations as well. The net result is more discord and violence, more broken relationships and broken communities than we have ever seen in our country. We are "not there yet," and we are not on our way to getting there because there is no real "there" to get to with modernism.

However, there is a way we can come close to being "there." By following timeless spiritual truths. By doing the things we know are right in our hearts. By looking beyond emotionalism and passing moral fads. By looking to the Author of life for strength and guidance. This will not bring about a perfect world; there will never be such a thing here on earth. But if we return to these principles, we can respond with strength and character to the calamities that are unavoidable. We can respond in a way that will bring us to the other side of trials stronger for the experience rather than weaker.

"If you don't know where you're going, you'll end up someplace else."
YOGI BERRA

ELEVEN

THE LESSER ANGELS OF OUR NATURES

"Let not our Liberty become license."
MARK TWAIN

HAVE WE LET our liberty become license? Have our freedoms worked toward our destruction? We have been free to choose our own leaders—but have we chosen leaders that will best govern and protect our country, or have we chosen "leaders" that will just cater to our self-centered and selfish desires, telling us what we want to hear and giving us what want? Self-governance requires self-restraint.

There are simple spiritual principles and guidelines for our lives that, if followed, will open up an outpouring of power and direction, a design for our lives that will bring harmony and integrity. Life then begins to make sense, and we begin to have purpose and strength and direction we would not have on our own. If an individual engages with these principles, it will bring blessings to him, those close to him, and those he comes in contact with. He will be an asset rather than a burden to those around him. He will be a giver, no longer obsessed with what is in it for him.

If a person rebels against or denies these principles, his or her life will be empty and devoid of real meaning or purpose. It may be masked by the substitutes for a real life: money, material things, vanity, sex, and endless entertainments and distractions, but in the end it will be a life spent in vain.

Some people seem more naturally inclined toward a life of contentment, direction, and security without consciously working at it. They lead lives of grace and purpose without striving. These people are very blessed.

The same spiritual principles that work to the benefit of an individual also work to bring about the best of society and governance. If we strive toward these principles, we have done what we can to further peace and prosperity in this world. The blessings may include material gains and economic prosperity, but more importantly it will bring about something of true brotherhood.

If we as a people deny these principles and rebel against their Author, we place ourselves on a very unstable footing. If we allow ourselves to be fooled and misled by charlatans that present a counterfeit offering of these principles, we are following a pied piper that will lead us to ruin.

All the greatest modernist leaders have presented themselves above all else to be benevolent and caring. In their way they presented themselves as spiritual leaders, as messiahs. They claimed to represent timeless and ascendant principles. If humanity had enough initial discernment when these ideas were first presented, the world could have been spared from such terrible violence and destruction. Now, however, we have the lessons of history. We can see what was promised, what was actually delivered, and what the consequences were. If we are wise and discerning now, we can look at what is being presented to us and compare it with recent history. The modernist's playbook has not changed since its inception. The personalities and languages may be different, but the story line remains much the same. Why should we expect the outcome to be any different? The definition of insanity is repeating the same behavior and expecting different results.

Being a counterfeit of real timeless spiritual principles, modernism cannot produce anything but terrible consequences. It can create a temporary state of apparent peace and prosperity, but it is only illusionary. Modernism, because it is based on man and materialism, deprives us of spiritual power and direction. It gives us a society that is fragmented, mean-spirited, and combative. It reduces people to waring tribal groups, causing them to tear at each other in order to get the governmental benefits they have been told they deserve. If they aren't fighting for financial remuneration, they will fight for the "rights" they have been led to believe are due them regardless of consequences for the world around them.

The expression "a wolf in sheep's clothing" usually brings to mind a cartoonish image of a fanged wolf with its tongue hanging out salivating while being poorly disguised by the sheep's cloak. We feel confident that if there are "wolves in sheep's clothing" among us, it will be that obvious to us. We think we will know right away that we are being fooled. The history of the past 150 years shows that we have not been so wise. It has shown us that modernist leaders can be incredibly cunning and diabolical in their persuasions. It has shown us that we can be incredibly gullible and easily led by modernist propaganda. Even when the evidence is plain that we have been fooled and destruction and catastrophe are at hand, many millions still cling to the illusion. We have many examples of these modernist empires rising with much glory and fanfare only to fold and collapse in a short time, all in vain. In spite of this evidence, modernism moves on as a great vanguard, still bringing destruction and death. In some places, a much more covert modernism proceeds apace, undermining all that makes for good society and true brotherhood.

Evil would not come to fruition if it was something simple and obvious. Evil would not take hold and become so pervasive and destructive in a culture if those entrusted with shining the beacon of truth were not somehow blinded to its realities.

In this age it is almost fatal for someone to suggest that there are inherent differences in races and people groups, but I believe an honest look would suggest that there are differences. We may all be equal, but our weaknesses and strengths are not equally balanced. Just like individuals have weaknesses and strengths, so do groups of people. Some groups may be more inclined to be stubborn and hardheaded, while others are overly compliant. Some may be more warlike and others more passive. Some are inclined to avarice; some to slothfulness. A more spiritual approach would be to admit and accept our weaknesses, work to correct them, and build on our strengths. People who are secure and love each other can freely confront each other about their weaknesses. They can also build each other up without being concerned about offending each other.

What modernists portray as diversity is really fragmentation—a type of tribalism that brings out the worst in us and pits us against one another.

Test of Character

When my daughter was six years old, she was diagnosed with type 1 diabetes, and she needed regular blood tests. This is now done with a finger prick and a drop of blood, but at the time it required a visit to a testing lab. This was fasting bloodwork, and she couldn't eat until after the test. The first time, we arrived at the lab early to try and beat the crowds. But being new to this, we didn't arrive early enough; there were at least fifteen people ahead of us in the waiting room, all college age and older. I quickly realized that it was going to be about three hours until my daughter's turn—three more hours without food or insulin for a six-year-old.

I approached the receptionist, and she told me she would see what she could do to move my daughter up the list. After a half hour, I checked with the receptionist again and realized that she was not doing anything. She then told me that if she let someone go ahead of the rest, the waiting room would erupt with complaints and anger. I was stunned. I couldn't believe that this group of well-dressed, educated, affluent adults would object to this consideration for a six-year-old girl.

The receptionist told me that before she could make an exception for my daughter, I would have to obtain permission from all the adults in the waiting room. No problem. I was still thinking that these adults would be happy to help my little girl out. I was wrong. For the most part my request was met with stony silence and some grumbling. The only person to speak up was a senior citizen who said, "What about me? I am diabetic too." This was one of the few times in my adult life that I was genuinely ashamed to be an American.

It is these little tests of character that reveal who we are as individuals and as a people. Most of those in that waiting room would probably consider themselves good people, but there is this snapshot in time that shows that perhaps that is not as true as we would like to think. Their own comfort was more important than that of a little girl.

Perhaps this is why healthcare that is controlled and administered by a centralized government is the Holy Grail of modernists. It is where we are most vulnerable, easily seduced, and controlled.

We are all prone to selfishness and self-centeredness, and the seductiveness of modernism is being told that our needs will be met with little or no effort on our part, that we are deserving and entitled. For almost every individual, family, race, trade union, gender, business, corporation, there has been some enticement to look to government for security. Perhaps it is impossible to live in our country and somehow not be drawn into some form of misplaced dependence on government.

It has been said that the end of civil government begins when the people realize they can vote themselves benefits from the public treasury by electing officials that will promise these benefits. Slaves to our own self-centeredness and fallen human nature, we then vote for the candidate that will increase these benefits the most until the treasury is bankrupt. At that time we reach "critical mass," the point when those who have resisted being seduced into being dependent on the state have been ensnared. We are then at a point where most of the electorate is dependent on the state. After that point, elections are only about which contestant will best sustain and increase those benefits. Some choose the apparently most liberal dispenser out of laziness and greed, others out of fear of losing what has become critical support for financial security, and still others out of pride and vanity, wanting to be part of this seemingly benevolent and morally superior movement. Because there aren't enough producers left to sustain the increases, the system is then manipulated, inflated, and drawn into massive debt followed by bankruptcy and collapse.

Some in our country think that it would be a good thing for the American nation to falter and fail. In their minds, we have been arrogant and need to be brought down. They are ignorant about what this would really look like or the immense suffering this would bring about. Historically, though, modernists have not been concerned about causing great suffering as long as it brings about the ends they desire. They are unconcerned with the suffering of others as long as their own power is maintained and increased. It is a kind of false humility to sabotage our own success and prosperity.

What would an empirical study of the effects and consequences of modernism reveal to us? What if we created a simple table that listed all the primary modernist political leaders and organizations of the past hundred years? It would be easy enough to jot down in one column a dozen such people or parties. We could list two or three from our own country and the balance from around the world. In the next column we could write a summary of what condition that country was in before they came to power, the state of the economy and of vital institutions like the family and the church. We could note how much debt there was. Next we could write what each person promised the outcome of their policies would be. This usually comes down to a few catch phrases. The third column could list who they blamed for the country's woes. (There is always a scapegoat in modernism). In the fourth column we could note what the state of the country was five, ten, twenty, forty, or sixty years after these changes had taken hold: the economic and social state of the country; how much conflict and strife; the spiritual state of the country, and so on. Did people care more or less for one another? In the government's treasury was there a healthy surplus or massive debt? How many innocents and combatants were killed or maimed by the ensuing conflicts? What groups provided support and what were their real motives?

If we were honest in filling out this table, I think that we would find the net result is that, in almost every case, there has been a decrease in real, solid economic security and much less brotherly love.

In many cases, there were real problems that required a solution. Perhaps the people and institutions that had real answers were either passive and did nothing or they had become corrupt and ineffective themselves. A solution was needed, but did the humanist, modern solution produce a net improvement in the lives of the people?

There have been apparent successes claimed by humanists. In our country, the left has laid claim to the advances in the civil rights movement. There was great progress, but, like other movements that started with right principles, it was corrupted by humanist ideals. Unable to establish equality of opportunity and then move on, an entitlement industry came into being. Instead of real spiritual principles that would provide the needed power to take hold of these opportunities, there was instead a seduction back into bondage of a different kind. What has been the net result? What was the state of black families before the sixties, and what is their state now?

As lofty as modernism appears, it simply has no lasting power to overcome or restrain the spiritual power of evil. With our own unaided vision, we are not even able to identify evil when it is squarely in front of us. Modernism is based on man's power, wisdom, and will, and therefore it is powerless to restrain evil. It boasts of doing great good, but in denying our fallen human nature, it is always destined to fail.

In some cases, the modernist leaders have been endorsed by those in positions of affluence and power, narcissistic children wanting to be aligned with a movement with an appearance of moral superiority, wanting to claim the moral high ground without any real humility.

There are many ways to measure the effects of modernism. It has reached into every nook and cranny of our lives, our culture, and our society. To keep it simple, we could look at two aspects of our lives that consume most of our time and energy, the two areas where we are the most insecure and frightened: financial and emotional security. Finance and romance. Security and sex. What has been the net return from our investment in modernist ideology in these two areas?

We all long to be accepted and loved as we are, to belong to something bigger than ourselves where we will be warmly embraced. We want to be financially secure and know that our needs will be met with a reasonable effort on our part. We want the opportunity to produce and enjoy the fruits of our labors. What an incredible level of corruption modernism has brought to these simple longings! Rather than security, modernism has brought fear, anxiety, and insecurity.

Modernists have exploited our primary fears for financial security and our need for emotional security by giving us a counterfeit of the real security we would find in these areas by turning to our Creator. As with all counterfeits, they are exposed for what they are in time.

Modernists have promoted their agenda through our fears and weaknesses, and they have hidden their agenda behind the weak— behind women and children the way terrorists conceal their munitions behind hospitals and orphanages.

As fallen creatures, we all have our own particular weaknesses. Some of us are more inclined to be lazy; some of us are more inclined to avarice. Some may be overly prudish while others may be inclined to licentiousness. The moral anarchy of modernism has removed the barriers and restraints Common Grace (the presence of God in our lives) would have otherwise provided. Common Grace is God's presence in our world whether we are consciously seeking him or not. It is His free gift, His unmerited favor, to mankind, that restrains us from further destroying ourselves even when we have wholly turned away from Him.

At an architectural seminar about growing our practices, the presentation started with this question: When did we become commoditized? This was during the depths of the recession. What they meant was: Under the financial stress of the economy, when did we stop being viewed as valued, trusted designers and advisors and become just a necessary project expense?

In the modernist world we could ask ourselves the same question. When did we become commoditized? When did we stop being thought of as individuals, spiritual beings and God's children, but instead let ourselves only be considered suppliers of votes and services and consumers of goods by the political and corporate classes? We have willingly let ourselves be manipulated into thinking we are fashionable, stylish, independent, and even radical, when in fact we have just been commoditized.

The truth is that every one of us was individually conceived in the heart and mind of our Creator before the earth was formed. Each of us has been given the gift of life on this earth at the time selected by Him for His purposes. Each of us is created in His image and likeness, precious and dearly loved in His sight far more than we can ever comprehend.

Who Gets the Blame?

We tend to blame God for all our problems. Even though many of us have never taken a moment to ask His direction, He still gets the blame. Modernists have certainly gone their way without ever sincerely looking to God for direction.

Historically, who are we keeping company with when we cast aspersions on the Church?

It is one thing to throw off the oppression of tyrannical men, but we discard the wisdom, guidance, and sustaining power of our Creator at our own great peril.

If we do think of Satan, it is usually in the same cartoonish way we imagine a wolf in sheep's clothing. Modernists tell us that Satan is just a superstition for simple-minded and uneducated people. The devil doesn't exist. If I were Satan, that is exactly how I would want people to think of me. I would want people to think that I didn't exist. I would want the purveyors of popular culture to tell everyone that only the simple minded, uneducated, and superstitious would believe in Satan—then I could carry out all my plans and be completely covert.

Along with an acknowledgement of our fallen nature, we need to acknowledge that there is evil in the world—there is a lower power that wants to destroy us. It is not so far-fetched when we look at the history of our civilization. The world has always been a flawed, violent, and tragic place. Humanist plans have only succeeded in making it much worse.

We have pushed God away, and then in our own flawed ways we have tried to cobble together and synthesize what comes naturally to Him.

Modernists have thought of themselves as benevolent, charitable courageous, and truthful. If they possessed these ideals, then their actions would bear fruit in kind. But instead the fruit has been more strife and the greatest destruction of innocent life in history.

Some talk of a punishing God. I am not a theologian, but I think of children, or young adults, that live in warm, loving, and functional homes. Like most functional homes, there are some rules to follow. Suppose these children decide they don't like these rules, and they rebel and run away. These young people may soon find themselves out living in the harsh elements and at the mercy of unscrupulous individuals. They may find themselves in physical and emotional pain and in very fearful circumstances. It is not that the parents are punishing their children—just the opposite. They are heartbroken and distraught, longing for their children to return to their love and protection. By their rebellion these children have taken themselves out from under the protection and care of their parents and are simply experiencing the natural consequences of their actions. They are leaving themselves exposed and unprotected from the evil in the world.

Again, I am not a theologian, but likewise I think God is not punishing us as a society. We are just experiencing the natural consequences of having taken ourselves out from under His protection. By rebelling and pushing Him aside, we are leaving ourselves exposed and unprotected from the evil that surrounds us in this world. Like the loving parents of the runaway children, He longs for us to return to His loving care and protection.

It's Not Too Late

Is it too late to turn things around? In the end, it is not really up to us but to the One that watches over us all, the One whose grace has sustained us and will continue to sustain us until His purposes are complete.

We have been prodigal children. We have taken an inheritance of freedom, prosperity, and abundance and turned it into a legacy of debt, dependence, and spiritual emptiness. The word *prodigal* simply means "wasteful." By turning back to simple, timeless truths what has been wasted can be restored. By returning to the loving and protecting arms of our Father-Creator, we can be healed and made whole again in all areas of our lives and culture.

"It is pride that changed angels into devils;
it is humility that makes men as angels."
St. Augustine

TWELVE

WHO WE COULD BE INSTEAD— A QUIET REVOLUTION

"Intelligence plus character—that is the goal of true education."
MARTIN LUTHER KING JR.

THE SAME QUALITIES and virtues that work for the happy, joyous, prosperous, and free life of an individual work for a family, a community, and a country. The beliefs and behaviors that revive and restore the life of an individual restore the life of a family, a community, and a culture.

If the characteristics that are bringing us down are *denial, dependence, debt*, and *decadence*, then the solution is simply the inverse of these: truth and acceptance, prudence and a modest approach to life, living within our means at all levels and all areas of life, dependence on God, appropriate self-sufficiency and real interdependence, and making brave, honest, and wise choices that will lift us all up.

In a time where every utterance in opposition to the modernist status quo is grossly distorted and subject to mob attacks, it is important that solutions be simple, tangible, and easier to defend against distortions.

Overcoming Denial

If life were easy—and it is not—it would be easy to see our faults, admit them to ourselves and others, and strive to correct them and do better. Then we would all be happy, joyous, and free, but as a society we are not. We can trace most of the trouble in our world to man's inability to acknowledge his faults and failures—or if you will, confess his sins. This is why pride is considered the greatest sin; it denies or justifies all others. Modernism has given this prideful denial of our fallen natures the credibility of "science" and "progress," and then codified the error in countless legislative actions. If there is no sin nor evil in the traditional sense, what is there to confess? If we deny the latent evil within us, then there are no battles to be fought and won—only rampant and unbridled human self-will. If an individual's life is dominated by self-will, he or she will trample on the lives of others, miss God's plan, and fail at life in a true and timeless way. If a society is propelled by the same kind of unbridled human "wisdom," it will not succeed, and the failure will be magnified by millions.

It should be fairly easy to see failed modernist policy, as it has always been characterized by the same three behaviors:

- Confiscation of private assets
- Control and micromanagement of the affairs of others
- Brutal treatment of innocent human life

To see through our denial, we have to be quiet in order to honestly assess where we are now. We must turn off the torrent of propaganda that inundates us every day from print and electronic media, with its cacophony of rationalizations, denials, and blame shifting. It is espoused at our schools and institutions or simply around the water cooler or from a bar stool. It emanates from a striated plinth on 8th Avenue and a cubist, gothic mid-rise on K Street NW. We must find the courage to turn away from this and honestly face our problems. Recent history has shown that we are not capable of doing this on our own; we need help—real help—from God. Otherwise we are just groping in the darkness while mistakenly thinking ourselves to be enlightened.

For real, honest, positive, change to occur, it requires deep conviction, not just a general sense that things are not as they should be. Too often, even in the face of the calamity and misery we've brought on ourselves, we refuse to depart from the destructive path we are on. Against a preponderance of evidence to the contrary, we insist that we are in the right and others are wrong. We might experience a tremendous sense of guilt and remorse, but still be undeterred. For a society or an individual, it requires a spiritual awakening and revelation to initiate real and lasting change, and this inner awakening requires God's grace. To receive this from Him, we simply need to humbly and collectively ask.

An alcoholic sometimes goes through times of binging and then pulls back until he returns to the good graces of family, friends, and employer. After a time the nightmarish memories fade, and he returns to his former ways. The downward cycle continues. Without conviction, the addiction progresses to its ultimate conclusion: incarceration, the collapse of his family, loss of financial viability, death.

Society can be like this. We see the economy suffer and the social chaos around us. In spite of the constant propaganda, we sense what the real problem is. For a period of time we choose leaders that hopefully will provide some moral clarity and fiscal responsibility. The symptoms subside for a while, and we return to the seductions of the modernist. We may look at the big picture and try to convince ourselves that things have turned around, but they haven't. Perhaps that is the nature of evil in the world, to have just enough evidence for us to convince ourselves that we are not in a state of decline when in fact we are.

To overcome denial we start with confession, which simply means to acknowledge our true faults and failings. Then we make an about-face, 180 degrees. We shake off our denial. We have all to some extent been modernists, loving to run amuck, have our own way, play God. We all want to be part of what's "cool," and none of us wants to be labeled as a repressive reformer. Doing the right thing at this time means going against the prevailing "wisdom" of our times. This is harder for those who are intellectually, morally, politically, or financially vested in the failing status quo.

To most of us, the word *apocalypse* conjures up images of great destruction, but the real meaning of the word is "revelation"—as in the all the faults and failings of a person, community, group of people, or nation revealed in one manifest, catastrophic failure and calamity. It is better, of course, to face the truth before it comes to that, before the truth is forced upon us in the ugliest and seemingly most cruel ways. The collapse of an empire is not pretty.

We have to admit that, when for the first time in history man has declared himself free of God and appointed himself supreme, it has not gone well. We have to admit, against protestations, that that is what we have done. Although couched in all manner of disguises, this has been the age of human "wisdom" and self-will.

It requires some un-modern virtues to turn this around: honesty that is not relative, situational, or "deconstructed"; courage and fortitude to stand up to the multitude of shrill voices that offer their convincing and seductive modernistic arguments.

This may seem like an impossible vision, but imagine all of our political leaders collectively admitting their failure of leadership and the monstrous mess they have made of our national finances. Of course they will never do this and therefore need to be told by the citizens of this country that they need to leave and turn over the job to those who are qualified to straighten things out.

Our Creator has given us a world in which there are always solutions before us. He allows difficulties and sometimes even great evil, but He never leaves us without hope and solutions. We simply need to admit our failure and acknowledge that we have traveled down a road that we shouldn't have. Simply having the humility to admit our error of near "cosmic proportions" will free us from the delusions we have believed in and give us a power not our own. The truth is so strong that it will open up reserves of strength to propel us forward into a future of real prosperity, peace within our borders, and true brotherhood.

Overcoming Dependence

It is not so much that we need to be free of all dependencies as we have to be free of morbid and misplaced dependencies and turn to dependencies that produce true freedom and prosperity. We have seen how inappropriate dependencies create debt and a kind of societal depression. We need to first turn to our Creator, the Author of life and the natural laws of the universe, for the guidance we need in helping those around us in distress.

Hope and a solution are closer for some than others. As the saying goes, "Ten miles into the woods, ten miles out of the woods." For people who have lived in the modernist message for generations, there is no point of reference when this message did not dominate every aspect of life. For some, there is no living memory of healthy, safe, peaceful, and vital communities without unreasonable government intrusion.

Even those of us that have such a reference are still limited by our own memories. We can read about the decline of other cultures. That is the value of non-revisionist history. Others who have been where we are can point the way to safety.

What works for the individual works for the world: Faith, hope, and charity; true brotherhood, not coerced; proverbial wisdom.

If we can be honest about the state that we are in, solutions will flow naturally from that point forward. This requires honesty regarding our real motives, the fact that we have tried to play God and it hasn't gone very well. One hundred years without God has left us in moral and spiritual destitution.

We need to speak of charity, but at the same time we need to speak honestly. We need to speak of prudence and wisdom at the same time. We need to honestly acknowledge that some individuals have been lazy and taken advantage of charity. Then we could acknowledge that "charity" might be more destructive to some than their current situation. We could acknowledge our limited human "wisdom" and turn to a source greater than ourselves. We need to love those whose lives are shattered by applying all the virtues of charity, honesty, and wisdom to start. This is how we truly restore lives.

Independence and healthy interdependence will restore our countries treasuries. Vastly more important than this, it will restore the sense of esteem and purpose of those that have been overly dependent, and, just as important, we can live in real "freedom, liberty, and brotherhood" as we won't be fighting each other so much over government spoils.

Finding Freedom from Debt

The solution to debt should be simple: Stop spending so much and begin paying down the debt. Modernist leaders, however, will go to great lengths to manipulate what should be a simple conversation.

When my wife and I were first married, we had debt that was not terribly significant, but it was enough to weigh on my mind. At the time, there were some programs on radio that stressed the importance of families living debt-free. We stumbled upon a book about getting out of debt that we would read out loud when traveling. The lessons sank in, and we began to live more frugally. We started with our smallest debts, such as department store credit cards. We moved on to paying down other cards, car loans, and student loans. We then started saving to pay off our mortgage in one lump sum. Once we got this momentum going, we were completely debt-free in a few years.

As my business grew, we grew our spending at a slower rate. We committed to living below our means. By doing so we were able to grow our savings and plan for future expenses that would come up. We have mostly bought used cars that served us well. We paid cash rather than burdening ourselves with debt just to impress others.

There were some sacrifices but nothing very significant. We drove old cars, turned the thermostat down, and put off discretionary spending. That was it—no bloodletting. The kids had everything they needed, and we still took vacations. Many families pile debt upon debt until it is unsustainable and all-consuming. What will undo a family will undo a nation. What works for a family will work for a nation.

There is a wonderful feeling walking up your driveway and thinking that the ground under your feet is paid for. It is liberating to be able to pay for everything in cash and to invest rather than borrow. Rather than fretting about unexpected expenses, we were able to set up an emergency fund for them. Our finances had a new momentum when we became debt-free.

It is very dispiriting to the working citizens of a country to have their hard-earned wages heavily taxed and then to see that tax revenue spent in ways that are wasteful, destructive and corrupting. But it's inspiring to the citizenry to see hard-earned wages used in wise and prudent ways. To give freely from your abundance to those in need is very gratifying. There is something perverse about "giving" from a position of great indebtedness.

It is really very simple. The same few steps our family took to get out of debt are the same that government needs to take. Not different—just on a larger scale.

Imagine the peace of mind we will experience living in a country without any debt, a country that has surplus. Imagine how much more useful and helpful our government will be when one-third of the tax revenue is not stolen away to pay for past excesses.

Reversing Decadence

Decadence is defined by Wikipedia as:

> The word *decadence*, which at first meant simply "decline" in an abstract sense, is now most often used to refer to a perceived decay in standards, morals, dignity, religious faith, or skill at governing among the members of the elite of a very large social structure, such as an empire or nation state. By extension, it may refer to a decline in art, literature, science, technology, and work ethics, or (very loosely) to self-indulgent behavior.
>
> Usage of the term frequently implies moral censure, or an acceptance of the idea, met with throughout the world since ancient times, that such declines are objectively observable and that they inevitably precede the destruction of the society in question. For this reason, modern historians use it with caution.

Elsewhere it is defined more simply as: "moral or cultural decline as characterized by excessive indulgence in pleasure or luxury."

All definitions of *decadence* have the common theme of decline. A decadent culture is in a state of descending rather than ascending.

It is interesting that Wikipedia goes on to say: "It bore the neutral meaning of decay, decrease, or decline until the late 19th century, when the influence of new theories of social degeneration contributed to its modern meaning." In other words, in a time of decadence the meaning of the word is denied or reinterpreted. The "new theories of social degeneration" are the ideas of modernism.

There really is not any neutral in life. We are either ascending, or we are descending and declining. We are either building a good society, or we are taking it down. Big decisions by leaders to choose decline and decadence over virtue are damaging. And the small decisions we make ourselves to choose *denial, debt, dependence,* and *decadence* over virtue are collectively damaging. Decadent people choose decadent leaders. We need to choose leaders that are not decadent in nature

A popular book back in the 1980s was titled *All I Really Need to Know I Learned in Kindergarten*. It described simple lessons of trust and guidelines for a good life. I would agree that the principles of a good life are simple—though not always easy to follow.

I might say, "All I really need to know I learned in the Boy Scouts." The Scout's Oath is also simple: "A Scout is Trustworthy, Loyal, Helpful, Friendly, Courteous, Kind, Obedient, Cheerful, Thrifty, Brave, Clean, and Reverent." There's nothing here that a reasonable person would find objectionable. It is simply a list of virtues that have stood the test of time. It may sound overly simplistic, but these are sound principles that can only bring good if applied to one's life. We can only benefit from choosing leaders that embody these characteristics rather than the modernist counterfeits.

Cynics among us may howl at the thought of it, but what works for a Boy Scout will work for a man, a family, a town a country. Yes, we need more Boy Scouts and Girl Scouts in public office.

The Way Forward

There is great freedom in facing the truth about ourselves. Shedding the mounting burden of years of deceiving ourselves paves the way for real hope and progress. Though it is scary, facing the truth will set in motion the gears of true change and transformation. Cutting loose the anchor of denial will put the wind back in our sails again. We will not have to settle for a synthetic, cobbled-together prosperity, but instead can experience a real, organic, bottom-up revival of what constitutes good governance and good society. We will not have to force equality but can have real fraternity. If we are capable of such honesty, some of our faulty constructions will simply recede on their own.

Independence and Interdependence

There are healthy forms of dependence that bring about a sense of freedom and vitality. Dependence on a loving God frees us from ourselves. Dependence on timeless precepts and virtues brings peace and civility back to our homes and main streets.

There is a difference between dependence and interdependence. Healthy interdependence requires everyone working together, humbly and freely giving according to his or her means, and those who are truly in need graciously accepting the help.

In a family, the adults protect and provide for the youngest and weakest. As the children grow, they assume more of a role of giving back to the family. We usually wouldn't have much respect for the adults or the children in a family where the parents continue to coddle their children into their adult years and the children never stop being takers.

In governance, this scenario of dependence plays out at all levels of the economic scale and every aspect of life. We have become used to the idea of an all-powerful government that will meet every crisis, every need, big and small. It is intimidating to think that we might have to stand or fall on our own. It requires extraordinary character for those who are dependent to resolve to take care of themselves as much as they can. It takes just as much strength and character for leaders to prudently meet real needs and not dole out cash and go into debt for political expediency and their own power base.

Abundance, Surplus, Prosperity

What liberty there is in being debt-free and giving out of one's abundance and surplus to those in need! There is virtue in giving from what you have gained from honest work and then serving others. Living within and below our means may seem boring, but it is true liberation.

Ascendance, VIrtue

Cadence is the balanced, rhythmic flow or the measure or beat of movement, life moving ahead in a steady flow. Decadence (de-cadence) is the opposite of that, fragmented and disoriented, not moving forward but stumbling backwards.

Decadence is the decline of a culture. Ascendance is the opposite of decadence. Ascendance is a natural outcome of a spiritually healthy people. This does not necessarily mean an ascendance in economic or military status, though it may.

If we have seen through our denials, chosen interdependence and *vital* dependencies rather than *morbid* dependencies. If we have resolved to reverse our fiscal and spiritual bankruptcy, ascendance will flow naturally from this.

A US president once said, "When the tide comes in, everyone's boat rises." He was speaking in economic terms, but the same could be said for the spiritual health of a nation. When the moral ideals are raised in word and deed by those in positions of influence, authority and responsibility then everyone's situation is improved except for the purveyors of vice and those that are vested in the problem.

If we uphold rather than scorn proven and timeless virtues and proverbial wisdom, then the benefits will ripple out to all. Neighborhoods blighted by modernism will be restored to peace.

As odd as some of them may appear, we need to listen to the prophets that are pointing out the dangers of our times. Real prophets throughout history have been the oddballs. The leaders that have brought about the most destruction have been the most charismatic, slick, polished, and nuanced. They have been the "cool ones."

Firmness, Utility, Delight

In closing, I come back to my love of architecture. Major architectural movements usually do not simply follow styles as we usually think of style. Some do, but the major movements have been outward manifestations of the beliefs of the time, in some ages more imperial in others more democratic. The social movements that produce architecture are not always positive, sometimes hedonistic and superficial, sometimes cold and spare. Sometimes architecture is as sublime and beautiful as the vital communities that inspire it. Sometimes as farcical as the decadent cultures it springs from.

As architecture records our history and social movements, so also ideals of architecture can provide direction and make practical applications to our lives and governance. In the same way a building needs a sound structure and solid building materials, a society requires a firm foundation of sound beliefs; societies built on the shifting sand of destructive and invasive ideologies cannot last. Buildings are only as strong as the materials used and the quality of the workmanship, and societies are the same. Societies built on ideas that are faulty or have failed in the past are weak and will not stand the test of time.

All good architecture that has stood the test of time follows Vitruvius' three principles: *firmness, utility,* and *delight.* All good governance that has stood the test of time follows these same principles. What works for good architecture works for good governance. *Firmness* is being based on sound ideas and timeless wisdom, not emotionalism, pride, and envy. *Utility* means fulfilling basic functions well and with economy. *Delight* is the result of a welcoming and free place for those that are of good will, those who truly seek to serve others, live peacefully, and give freely.

There is a collection of architectural design books that were popular among students in the 1970s called *The Timeless Way of Building.* The books are about beautiful "living" architecture that was mostly rural, indigenous and organic—brought about by local, vital communities before the advent of modernism. There is also a timeless way of living and governance that can come about from local, vital communities.

As a nation we are off track in many areas, but there are simple solutions to our problems. We cannot expect the necessary leadership to come from political leaders of either stripe. Instead we need to individually and collectively work to restore our nation's vitality and freedom.

Modernism and its leaders are not going away anytime soon, but we can diminish their power and mitigate their destructiveness. While this world was never meant to be a utopia, we can reverse the course and start to build a healthy and vital society again.

We can aspire to and practice higher ideals, ones that are true and tested. This is the best we can hope for in this fallen world—to be reasonably happy, free, and prosperous. To build our culture, strength, and reserves to meet challenges, big and small, that will come to us. We can be ready for them if we change.

We don't need a revolution or a massive movement. We just need a small percentage of people to start doing the right thing. This would be enough to tip the scales back in the right direction.

We really have gotten far away from being our true selves over the past few generations. We have come to be characterized by extreme self-centeredness. Now, with God's help, we can become ourselves again and revive the "better angels of our natures."

We can be forgiven, but we cannot continue as we have without dire consequences.

Forgiveness needs to be at the heart of any recovery. Seeking God's forgiveness for the terrible mess we have made of this culture that was gifted to us. Forgiving ourselves and others for real or imagined past hurts and injustices. Exercising forgiveness toward those that have been the primary promoters and supporters of modernism. We have a national day of Thanksgiving on the fourth Thursday in November. Perhaps we should have a National Day of Forgiveness. I would propose the second Thursday in November since it is fitting that one should come before the other.

I have heard it said that when men go mad, it is en masse. When they begin to return to sanity, it is one at a time. Let's start the walk back, each of us on our own, and hopefully together as well.

Together we all need to offer up that simple earnest prayer: "Help!" If we do we are certain to find that God is not dead, but that He is alive, and He cares for us in ways we have not imagined. Then, acting in true humility, honesty, wisdom, courage, faith, hope, and charity will save the day!

May we have that needed humility, honesty, wisdom, courage, faith, hope, and charity in our time, and may our Heavenly Father deliver us from the evils of modernism..

"Then pealed the bells more loud and deep:
"God is not dead, nor doth He sleep:
The Wrong shall fail,
The Right prevail,
With peace on earth, good-will to men"
RALPH WALDO EMERSON

"On the other hand, perhaps it is possible, especially in strange times
such as these, for an entire people, or at least a majority, to deceive
themselves into believing that things are going well,
when in fact they are not, when things are in fact farcical.
Most Romans worked and played as usual while Rome fell about their ears."
WALKER PERCY, THE SECOND COMING